JOYFULLY

BRIAN L. HARBOUR

BROADMAN PRESS
NASHVILLE, TENNESSEE

©Copyright 1991 ● Broadman Press
All rights reserved
4210-12
ISBN: 0-8054-1012-0
Dewey Decimal Classification: 227.6
Subject Heading: BIBLE N.T. PHILIPPIANS - SERMONS
Library of Congress Catalog Card Number: 90-22974
Printed in the United States of America

Library of Congress Cataloging-in-Publication Data

Harbour, Brian L.

    Living joyfully / Brian L. Harbour.

      p. cm. -- (Living the New Testament faith)

    Includes bibliographical references.

    ISBN 0-8054-1012-0

    1. Bible. N.T. Philippians--Commentaries. I. Title.

II. Series.

BS2705.3.H368 1991

227'.607--dc20

                                    90-22974
                                        CIP

Dedicated to my church family at
First Baptist Church,
Richardson, Texas,
who love God's Word

Preface

A couple was at a football game. The weather was horrible. The temperature was below twenty degrees. Sleet and snow had been falling since the game began. The woman became sick after eating some popcorn. Three men sitting behind the couple repeatedly spilled their drinks on them. Their team was behind forty to nothing. The wife turned to her husband and said, "Now, Honey, tell me again how much fun we're supposed to be having!"

Many Christians are like that woman. They go through life overcome by circumstances, never really experiencing the joy of the abundant life Christ wants to give us. They live under their circumstances instead of rising above them to find true joy.

How different from the apostle Paul. Paul had problems like we do today. He was constantly harassed, often beaten, and normally misunderstood. He would jump out of the frying pan only to land in the fire! He spent many years in prison because of his commitment to Christ. Yet, a spirit of joy permeated his life. In no other letter did Paul so clearly reveal the source and substance of his joy than in the Philippian Epistle. It is indeed the epistle of joy. My prayer is that, as you read this testimony of joy which Paul wrote to the Philippians, you will discover the secrets of Paul's life and apply them to your life so you, too, can begin *Living Joyfully.*

Contents

1 | With Love from Paul

Philippians 1:1-2

One of the most delightful books in my library is entitled, *Dear Pastor,* by Bill Adler. It contains letters written by children of various ages to their pastor.

One of the letters from eleven-year-old Ralph said, "Dear Pastor, I liked your sermon on Sunday. Especially when it was finished."

A letter from ten-year-old Anthony said, "Dear Pastor, I would like you to marry me and my girlfriend when we get married someday." Then he added this postscript, "I'll let you know when I find a girlfriend."

Nine-year-old Susan wrote, "Dear Pastor, Please say a prayer for my teacher. She is sick and if you said a prayer, she would get better and come back to school." Susan added this postscript, "The other kids in my class said I shouldn't write this letter."[1]

Nothing is more enjoyable than reading a letter from a friend you've not seen in a while, from a child who is living in another city or away at school. A letter is an intimate expression of the feelings and desires and interests of that person.

Philippians is a personal letter written by the apostle Paul to his friends in the city of Philippi. What makes this letter special is that its contents were inspired by God and it has been included in the New Testament as a part of our Scriptures. As we study this letter we will discover the insights and challenges given to these Christians in the first century are also relevant and applicable to us today. We learn about the author of this letter in the opening verses.

Paul: The Author (1:1)

Who was this Paul who penned the Philippian Epistle? He was a devout Jew who at one time saw Christianity as a threat to the true faith, so he dedicated himself to destroying those who claimed to be followers of Christ. However, on his way to Damascus to persecute the Christians he had a dramatic encounter with Jesus Christ, an event told about in Acts 9, 22, and 26. In that dramatic Damascus road experience, Paul was transformed from an apostle of the Sanhedrin into an apostle of Jesus Christ.

Paul then traveled all over the known world, planting churches and proclaiming Christ. Finally, he was arrested by the Jewish leaders because the new faith he propagated conflicted with their understanding of God. Their intention was to put him to death. To save his life, Paul used his prerogative as a Roman citizen to appeal to Rome. Thus, he was sent to Rome for the final decision concerning the charges against him. While in prison in Rome, around AD 63, Paul penned this letter to the Philippians.

Notice Paul's name does not stand alone at the beginning of this epistle. We also see the name of Timothy. Timothy was a young man who became Paul's companion and at times his emissary. In the two letters Paul later wrote to Timothy, he referred to this young co-worker as his "true child in the faith" (1 Tim. 1:2). Timothy is mentioned twenty-four times in the New Testament. Why are both Paul and Timothy's names mentioned at the beginning of this letter? Does this mean they coauthored this letter? No, because after the greeting, Paul immediately spoke in the first person singular in verse 3, "I thank my God in all my remembrance of you." And he referred to Timothy in 2:19-24 in the third person.

If Timothy was not the coauthor of this letter, why did Paul include his name at the beginning of it? Probably because of Timothy's association with the church at Philippi. Timothy was associated with Paul in bringing the gospel to the Philippians (Acts 16:11-40). He visited them on more than one occasion (Acts 19:21-22; 20:3-6). And he would be sent to them again later (Phil. 2:19-23). So Paul wanted to affirm his confidence in Timothy and to confirm that he and Timothy represented the same cause. Paul and Timothy were co-workers in the proclaiming the same gospel.

Paul: The Servant (1:1)

In the opening verse of his Epistle to the Philippians, Paul identified himself as a servant of Christ Jesus. Paul did not call himself an apostle as he did in the Roman letter. There, the nature of the letter demanded a declaration of his authority and position. In this case, however, the extraordinary trust between Paul and those to whom he wrote in Philippi made such a designation superfluous. I would not go home in the afternoon and announce to my children, "This is Dr. Brian Harbour, pastor of the First Baptist Church in Richardson. I'm home!" Nor did Paul need to make that kind of announcement. He simply called himself a servant of Jesus Christ.

Several Greek words can be translated into the English word "servant." A *diakonos* was a servant who ministered. A *therapon* was an attendant. An *oiketes* was a house servant. A *misthios* was a hired servant. None of those is the word used here. The word used here is *doulos* which literally means bondslave. A *doulos* is one in a relationship to another which only death can break. Paul suggested the one most descriptive word which explained his relationship to the Lord was the word, "slave." He was a bondslave of Jesus Christ.

To the Greeks, this idea would have been intolerable. To the Jewish rabbis, to call someone a *doulos* (slave) was one of the worst insults you could hurl at a man, an undesirable epithet. Yet, Paul deliberately and proudly referred to himself as a slave of Jesus Christ.

What does it mean to be a slave of Jesus Christ?

Identified with His Master

The word translated *slave* has its derivation from a word that means to bind. A slave was bound to or inseparably connected to another. His whole identity was derived from the one to whom he belonged.

This is what Paul meant when he called himself a slave of Jesus Christ. He was no longer his own. He had been bought with the blood of Jesus Christ, and now he belonged to Him (1 Cor. 6:20). His whole life pointed to Christ and his total identity was found in Christ. He was identified with Him.

Obedient to His Master

In Matthew's Gospel, we read about a Roman centurion, an army officer, who came to Jesus. He was a man with authority over his forces. He told Jesus, "For I, too, am a man under authority, with soldiers under me; and I say to this one, 'Go!' and he goes, and to another, 'Come!' and he comes, and to my slave, 'Do this!' and he does it."(Matt. 8:8-9).

What a beautiful picture of our relationship to Christ. He is the head of the church and the Lord of the Christian. That means He has authority over our lives. To call ourselves His slave means that we are obedient to Him.

Supplied by His Master

For all the bad aspects of the institution of slavery, slavery had one distinct benefit. The slave had no worries about his supplies. His clothes, his food, his medical treatment, his housing—everything was provided by his master.

To be a slave of Jesus Christ brought a sense of contentment to Paul's heart, for he knew he could rely on Christ for all his resources. Paul expressed this idea clearly near the end of this letter to the Philippians when he said, "My God shall supply all your needs according to His riches in glory in Christ Jesus" (Phil. 4:19).

Paul was a servant of Jesus Christ, identified with Him, obedient to Him, provided for by Him.

Paul: the Pastor (1:1-2)

We see a third picture of Paul. He was also a pastor to the people of Philippi. With the heart of a pastor, Paul spoke to the members of the church at Philippi.

A Word of Challenge (1:1)

Paul identified those to whom he wrote as saints. The word translated saints is *hagiois*. Today the word *saint* is not usually a compliment. We say it like this: "That's Jane Johnson. She thinks she is such a saint." Paul, however, did not use the term in a derogatory sense but to clearly designate what a Christian is. The word *saint* is used over sixty times in this way in the New Testament. The word literally means "set aside" or "sanctified." Saints are unholy people who have been singled out, claimed, requisitioned, and then set aside by God for His control and use. The word *saint* clarified three things about the Philippian Christians.

The word saint declared the root of their lives.— These Christians at Philippi could be called saints, not because they were perfect, not because they were without sin, not because they were better than everybody else but because they were "in Christ Jesus." They were ordinary people to whom something extraordinary had happened. They were common people whose lives had linked up with an uncommon Savior. They were saints because they were "in Christ Jesus."

Notice these saints were also "in Philippi." They were not isolated from the world. They did not live in a Christian subdivision physically set apart from the world. They lived in the world, in the city of Philippi, in the midst of an unclean and sinful world, but they were saints because they were also in Christ.

Saints are reared in unlikely neighborhoods. A saint can live anywhere, as long as he is in Christ. A saint can come from any neighborhood as long as he is in Christ. Although Philippi was the sphere of the Philippians' lives, it did not provide the root of their lives. They were at Philippi but in Christ Jesus. Their lives were rooted in Christ.

The word saint defined the responsibility of their lives.—Because the Philippians had been set apart for a special purpose, they needed to live as the special people they were. Something is wrong with a prince who lives like a pauper. Something is wrong with an adult who behaves like a child. Likewise, something is wrong with a saint who does not act like a saint, a Christian who does not talk or act like a Christian. We are not only to be saints in name but also saints in fact.

What a tremendous impression would be made upon the world if we Christians acted like the saints we are supposed to be!

The word saint described the reward of their lives.—Saint and sanctification come from the same root and describe not only our responsibility but also our reward. Paul gave the Philippians this word of hope: "For our citizenship is in heaven, from which also we eagerly wait for a Savior, the Lord Jesus Christ; who will transform the body of our humble state into conformity with the body of His glory" (3:20-21).

A little girl with a deformed physical body often received ridicule and mockery from her classmates. One afternoon she crawled into her mother's lap when she came home from school. "Mom," she asked, "why did

God make me like this?" Her mother wisely responded, "God is not through making you yet!"

The promise of God's word is that someday we will not only be saints in name but also saints in fact.

A Word of Commendation (1:1)

Paul specified two groups among the saints for a special word of commendation: the overseers and the deacons.

The Greek word translated *overseers* is the word *episkopois*. Most scholars conclude the word translated *overseer* (*episkopos*) and the word translated *elder* (*presbuteros*) are used as synonyms in the New Testament. (Acts 20:17, 28 and 1 Pet. 5:1-2). Both refer to the office of pastor.[2]

The Greek word translated *deacon* is the word *diakonois*. This word means a servant or a minister. The word was used in a general way at times to refer to a follower of Christ. It was also used in a technical, official way to speak of the office of deacon originated in Acts 6. It is obviously used in this technical, official way here.

Why did Paul mention the overseers and the deacons when he expressly stated this letter was to all the saints who were in Philippi? Apparently these leaders had taken the initiative in gathering the gifts sent to Paul by the Philippians and he wanted to thank them. Paul was giving to them a word of commendation as he singled them out in the introduction of the letter.

A Word of Comfort (1:2)

Paul expressed to the Philippians the greeting with which he normally opened his epistles. Paul said, "Grace to you and peace from God our Father and the Lord Jesus Christ." "Grace" is what the Greeks said when they greeted one another in Paul's day. "Peace" is what the Hebrews said when they greeted one another in Paul's day. As an heir of both cultures, Paul combined the two and said, "Grace to you and peace." This greeting is a compact expression of Paul's entire message. What did this greeting mean?

Paul reminded the Philippians of the richness of God's grace.—What is grace? Grace is God's riches at Christ's expense. Grace is what man needs but does not deserve. Grace is the merciful nevertheless with which God steps out from the mystery of His majesty and holiness and turns to address mankind. Grace is God's active favor by which He bestows His greatest gift on those who deserve the greatest punishment. Grace is, as Martin Luther once said, "God's middle name."

Paul wanted these Christians at Philippi to experience the fullness of God's grace, to allow God to be as good to them as He wanted to be.

Paul reminded the Philippians of the results of God's grace.— What is peace? Peace is that which comes as a result of God's grace. Because of God's grace, we know our past is pardoned by God, and that gives us a sense of peace. Because of God's grace, we know our present is empowered by God, and that gives us a sense of peace. Because of God's grace, we know our future is secure in God, and that gives us a sense of peace.

Paul wanted the Philippians to experience real peace, the kind that is made available through God's grace. This kind of peace is an inner tranquility in the midst of outer turmoil, a peace which derives from the fact that we are a part of God's forever family and the knowledge that God has the whole world in His hands and under His control, a peace which emanates from the assurance that "neither death, nor life, nor angels, nor principalities, nor things present, nor things to come, nor powers, nor height, nor depth, nor any other created thing, shall be able to separate us from the love of God, which is in Christ Jesus our Lord" (Rom. 8:38-39).

When Paul thought of these Christian friends in Philippi whom he loved so dearly, the desire of his heart was not that they might have health, wealth, or prestige. His desire was that they might be comforted by the grace and peace of God.

Paul reminded the Philippians of the revealer of God's grace.—Where does this grace and peace come from? Paul explained in verse 2. Grace and peace will come "from God our Father and the Lord Jesus Christ." Notice Paul connected God the Father and God the Son and spoke of them as being equal. The Father is the source from whom grace and peace come. The Son is the Person through whom they come. Grace and peace come from God. We obtain these blessings and experience them through Jesus Christ.

These two verses introduce Paul, the author, the servant, and the pastor, and they set the stage for our study of the Philippian Epistle.

For Discussion

1. Read Paul's conversion experiences in Acts 9, 22, and 26. In what ways was your conversion experience similar to Paul's? In what ways was it different?

2. Apply the idea of being a servant of Christ to your life. In what ways can we identify with Christ today? In what areas do we need to be obedient to Christ today? What needs are supplied by Christ today?

3. Do you like being referred to as a saint? If not, why not? What are some positive meanings of that word?

4. Who are some individuals who positively contributed to your Christian life?

5. Contrast the biblical meaning of peace with the common understanding of peace.

2 | The Praying Apostle

Philippians 1:3-11

One of the great men of prayer in Christian history was George Mueller (1805-1898) who spent his life in the service of Christ in London. After a dissolute early life, he was converted during a prayer meeting in 1825. Mueller came to London in 1829 to train for missionary service among the Jews. He decided to stay in England and eventually focused his attention on the needs of children. He established an orphanage in Bristol which grew from a rented house into a great complex of buildings. He renounced a regular salary and refused throughout the rest of his life to make any requests for financial support either for himself or for his philanthropic projects. He depended entirely on prayer. He kept a notebook with two-page entries. On one page he gave the petition and the date. On the opposite page he entered the date of the answer. Mueller testified that in his lifetime 50,000 specific prayers were answered. Prayer was the secret of George Mueller's productive life for Christ.[1]

The apostle Paul was also a man of prayer. Paul's prayer for the Philippians revealed some important insights about his attitude toward life and his relationship with God.

Paul's Thankfulness (1:3-6)

For what are we most thankful? Some of us may say we are most thankful for our friends who have helped us to make it through life. William Barclay, gifted British scholar, wrote in his autobiography he was thankful that being such as he was he had the friends that he had.[2] Or perhaps you are most thankful for the challenges of life which have helped you to become a better person. Helen Keller expressed her testimony in these words: "I thank God for my handicaps for through them I have found myself, my work and my God." Or your gratitude might be very practical like the little boy who said, "I'm thankful for my glasses, for they keep the boys from hitting me and the girls from kissing me."

Thankfulness permeated the heart of the apostle Paul. As in all his epistles, except the letter to the Galatians and the personal epistle to Titus, Paul followed his greeting with hearty words of thanksgiving: "I thank my God in all my remembrance of you" (v. 3). These words of thanksgiving expressed the heart of the apostle Paul. Paul had a Hallelujah Chorus in his heart. Paul thought of the Philippians with an attitude of gratitude.

Paul's expression of thanksgiving is especially remarkable when we remember what actually happened in Philippi when Paul was there. After Paul healed the slave girl in Philippi, "her masters saw that their hope of profit was gone" so "they seized Paul and Silas and dragged them into the market place before the authorities" (Acts 16:19). Yet, Paul could say, "I thank my God in all my remembrance of you."

While Paul and Silas were in Philippi, "The chief magistrates tore their robes off them, and proceeded to order them to be beaten with rods. And when they had inflicted many blows upon them, they threw them into prison" (Acts 16:22-23). Yet, Paul could say, "I thank my God in all my remembrance of you."

When Paul and Silas were arrested, the jailer "threw them into the inner prison, and fastened their feet in the stocks" (Acts 16:24). Yet, Paul could say, "I thank my God in all my remembrance of you."

Paul's thankfulness can only be comprehended when we focus on the two key words in verse 3: God and you. Paul could be thankful, even in the midst of unfavorable circumstances, because he served a God who had everything under control. Because God was bigger than any problem, Paul could always say, "I thank my God." The other key word is "you." Paul was not thankful for the happenings in Philippi, but for the people with whom he shared those happenings. That's the bottom line of this attitude of gratitude. Paul was not thankful for suffering. He was not thankful for his hard times in Philippi. He was thankful for the Christians in Philippi who were his brothers in Christ.

Why was Paul thankful every time he remembered the Philippians (v. 3)? Why, when he prayed for them, did he pray with joy (v. 4)? Two reasons appear in our text.

Because of What They Had Done for God (1:5)

Paul thanked God for the Philippians because of their "participation in the gospel." The word translated "participation" is *koinonia*. We usually think *koinonia* means "fellowship." However, it means so much more than that. This word speaks of a covenant between two people, a partnership. In some of the ancient papyri, the word *koinonia* was used to speak of a marriage contract, and on other occasions it spoke of a commercial partnership. In Luke 5:10, James and John were described as "partners with Simon." The word "partners" is *koinonoi*. In 2 Corinthians 8:23, Paul called Titus "my partner." The Greek word is the word *koinonos*. *Koinonia* is more than fellowship. It is a working partnership. It is an agreement between two parties who are committed to a common task. It means participation in something. Paul was thankful for the Philippians because of the characteristics displayed in their participation in the gospel.

Paul was thankful for their initiative.—Paul said the Philippians participated in the gospel "from the first day." From the very first day Paul arrived in Philippi, when Lydia opened her home to him (Acts 16:15), they participated in the work of the gospel. They were not hesitant. They were not slow starters. They immediately responded and got involved.

A pastor in a small town went down to the train station every day and watched the train come roaring through. One of his deacons asked him why he followed that same ritual every day. The pastor responded, "That's the only thing moving in this town that I don't have to push." Paul did not have to push the Philippians. They were self-starters. They had initiative. They started well.

Paul was thankful for their persistence.—Paul said the Philippians also finished well. He said they participated in the gospel "from the first day until now." They did not give up when the going was tough. They were not quitters. They didn't fizzle out at the finish. They didn't go up like rockets and then come down like rocks. They began well, and then they finished well.

A modern-day model of persistence was Dr. Gaines S. Dobbins. He was the first dean of the School of Religious Education at The Southern Baptist Theological Seminary. After spending forty years on the faculty at Southern, he retired by going to Golden Gate Seminary, where he served another fifteen years. At the age of eighty he retired again from Golden Gate Seminary and moved to Birmingham. He became chaplain of the retirement home where he lived and became an active Sunday School worker in Shades Mountain Baptist Church. During those years he continued to teach through Boyce Bible School. Then, when he was eighty-nine years old, he wrote a book entitled, *Zest for Living.* When he was ninety, he spoke at the convocation at Southern Seminary, addressing the theme, "The Next 20 years in Theological Education." When he died, they found a page of paper in his typewriter, half finished, as a part of yet another book he was writing. He abided in Christ until the very end.[3] The church at Philippi was full of saints who started well and finished well and Paul was thankful for them.

Because of What God Was Going to Do for Them (1:6)

The work God was doing in the Philippians was the work of salvation. This verse reveals some simple but significant truths about the experience of salvation.

It was God's work.—Paul said the work being done in the lives of the Philippians was God's work. Paul did not begin the work in them, nor did the Philippians themselves. It was God. The spiritual transformation in the life of an individual is something only God can do. It is His work.

It was a good work.—Paul said the work God was doing in the Philippians was good in origin, quality, purpose, and results. When we allow God to do His work in our life, the results will be good. What God can do for us is always better than what we can do for ourself.

It was a continuing work.—Paul said the good work God had begun in the Philippians He would complete. God finishes what He starts. That which He redeems, He preserves to the very end. Paul said God will keep working in our lives until the day of Christ Jesus. The second coming of Jesus Christ is one of the clearest and most important doctrines of the New Testament. Paul never set a date for it, but he was certain it would occur. Someday Jesus is coming again. God is going to keep on working on us and shaping our lives until that day when we see Christ face to face and we will become like Him.

Paul's Love (1:7-8)

What we normally refer to as four-letter words are not the kinds of words you use in a church, nor do they appear in the Bible. They are scratched on fences and walls as obscene graffiti. However, one four-letter word is found all the way through the Bible. In fact, it is the theme of the Bible—*love*. Love was one of Paul's favorite words. Therefore, it is not surprising that in the opening verses of this personal epistle to the Philippians, Paul again expressed this theme.

After his greeting to the Philippians, Paul told them in verse 3 he had them constantly on his mind. In verse 7, Paul took it a step further and said he not only had them on his mind. He also had them on his heart. The word for heart is *kardia*, the word from which we get our word *cardiac*. The New Testament use of the word *kardia* focused more on the psychic and spiritual life. That is, the heart was considered the center of a person's inner life, the source of all the forces and functions of soul and spirit. The heart was the source of the feelings, emotions, desires, and passions of human life. Therefore, when Paul said to the Philippians, "I have you in my heart" (v. 7), he confessed that his deepest feelings, emotions, desires, and passions were directed toward them. Paul loved the Philippians with a deep and abiding love. Paul's love for the Philippians was something that could be neither discouraged nor disguised.

It is easier to talk about love than to express it truly. It is one thing to know we should love one another but another to do it. An old quip suggests it would be easier to love our neighbors if they weren't our neighbors. It was no easier for Paul than for us. Paul was human, just as we are. Paul could be hurt, and, in fact, was hurt, by some in Philippi. Some obnoxious people were members of the church at Philippi, just as there are in our churches today. How then could Paul say to all of the Christians at Philippi "I love you"? We see two answers to that question in our text.

Because of the Cause to Which They Were Committed (1:7)

The word "partakers" is a derivative of the Greek word *koinonia*. Paul added the prefix *sun*, which means "with" to emphasize the fact that the Philippians were partners together with him, that they were in this thing together. The Philippians' commitment to a common cause smoothed away their differences, softened their obnoxious qualities, and molded them together into a unit.

One of the most remarkable examples of this phenomenon in my own personal life happened several years ago when I coached my son Marty and fourteen other seven-year-old boys on a soccer team called Solid Gold. Our record that year was 20-0. We scored 173 goals, more than eight goals a game, and we had only one goal scored against us, in the very last game of the season. We ended up winning that game 9-1. I saw a remarkable thing with that team all season long. They were all very athletic and very aggressive. Practice times were a constant test of my patience. The boys picked at each other, fought with each other, and competed against each other during practice. They were a real pain. But on game day something happened. When Solid Gold ran out onto the field and the whistle blew, they became a team committed to a common purpose. They wanted to win. That was their purpose. They passed to each other, and encouraged each other, and helped each other in a remarkable demonstration of love that transcended all their differences and petty rivalries. Their love was generated by their united commitment to a common cause.

That is the kind of love Paul talked about in verse 7, a love which grew out of a partnership of cooperative commitment. That needs to happen to our churches today. Christians need to love each other. We need to have each other "in our heart."

How can we do that with so many differences among us, differences in background and social status and age? How can we have that kind of love for each other? Here is the answer. When we focus our attention on a common goal, to build growing, dynamic churches for Jesus Christ, when we forget everything else except our commitment to that one goal, then we will begin to experience that kind of love.

Because of the Christ to Whom They Were Committed (1:8)

The word translated "affection" is the Greek word *splagchnois*, which was used for the nobler internal organs such as the heart, liver, and lungs, as opposed to the lower intestines or bowels. The word referred to strong feelings. Paul loved the Philippians with "the affection of Christ Jesus."

What did Paul mean by that statement? Paul's love for the Philippians found its source not within him but literally within Jesus Christ. Paul was not talking about his love channeled through Christ. He was talking about Christ's love channeled through him.

How can we have others on our heart? How can we really love all Christians? Here is the answer. We need to allow the love of Christ to flow through us. We do not need to conjure up our own feelings within us. We need to allow Christ's feelings to channel through us.

Years ago a man was found unconscious on the street and was brought to a private hospital for care. Upon regaining consciousness, he began to abuse everyone who came to his room to minister to him. Finally, only one nurse would go near the difficult patient. She alone endured the foul language, bathed him, changed the linens, and brought his meals. On a Friday, the nurse came early and told the patient she would be leaving to go to a retreat. She told him she would miss taking care of him over the weekend. The man explained he would not be there when she returned. He was being taken to a charity hospital. "Since this is good-bye," he said, "will you explain to me why you continued to take care of me despite my behavior and bad language, when no one else bothered with me?" The nurse responded, "I believe that God loves you, and He may want to love you through me."

That was the secret of Paul's love for the Philippians. It was not his love at all. It was the love of Christ Jesus flowing through him. Paul believed Jesus Christ loved the Philippians, and He wanted to love them through Paul.

A reporter once asked Mother Teresa how she measured the success and failure of her work. She said she did not think God used categories like success and failure. The measurement instead was this: "How much have you loved?" That's a good question for each of us to ask ourselves.

Paul's Desire (1:9-11)

In the Old Testament period, the Hebrew high priest wore a costly shoulder garment called an ephod which hung over his heart. Over the ephod was the breast piece. The breast piece contained twelve precious stones, set in gold, with the names of the twelve tribes of Israel engraved upon them. The high priest wore these garments whenever he performed his priestly duties. The priest literally carried the people on his heart when he went into the holy place to pray to the Lord (Ex. 28:15-30).[4] In the same way, Paul lovingly carried the names of the Philippians on his heart. He cared for them (v. 7) and longed for them (v. 8) with a deep, abiding love.

When we love someone we want the best for them. When we want the best for someone, we will pray for them. So the passion of verses 7-8 led to the petitions of verses 9-11. Paul's concern for the Philippians led him to pray for four specific things.

A Fuller Experience of Love (1:9)

What kind of love did Paul have in mind in verse 9? Some see this as a reference to the love the Philippians were to have for each other. That is, Paul prayed the Christians in Philippi would get along better with each other, that their fellowship would be strengthened, that their love for each other would be deepened. Jesus certainly admonished His followers to love one another (John 15:12). And Paul wrote to the Thessalonians, "And may the Lord cause you to increase and abound in love for one another" (1 Thess. 3:12). In addition, one of the problems of the Philippians was some bickering in the fellowship (2:1-3;4:2), so they needed to grow in their love one for another. While all of those things were true, Paul was not talking about their love for each other but their love for God. Paul wanted the Philippians to have a deeper love for God so they would be able to endure more for His sake. He wanted them to have a wider love for God so they would be able to embrace more for His kingdom. He wanted them to have a fuller love for God so they would risk more for His will.

That the Philippians already loved God was evident in their lives. Paul prayed this love might abound still more and more, that it might flow in abundance, that it might show a great increase. He wanted the Philippians to have a fuller experience of the love of God.

A Finer Evaluation of Life (1:10a)

Paul wanted the Philippians to "approve the things that are excellent." The Greek word translated "approved" (*dokimazein*) means to put something through the test with a view toward approving it. This word was used for assaying metals to determine their worth. The Greek word translated "excellent" (*diapheronta*) literally means "things that differ," things that pull in opposite directions. So Paul was praying that these

Christians at Philippi would be able to apply spiritual tests to the different views, appeals, attitudes, and actions around them and discern which ones were best, which ones really had value.

The Phillips translation puts Paul's phrase like this: "I want you to be able always to recognise the highest and the best." Moffatt translates verses 9-10 to say, "It is my prayer, . . . enabling you to have a sense of what is vital."

What a need for our day! Every day we face myriads of choices not just between good and bad, but also between good and better and between better and best. More than anything else today we need a sense of what is vital, a spiritual sensitivity to true value so we will be able to distinguish between the good and the best and, thus, give our approval to those things that are excellent.

How can we get this sense of what is vital? How will we be able to discern between the good and the best? This second element of Paul's prayer grows naturally out of the first. We develop spiritual discernment by abounding more and more in our love for God. The more we love God, and the closer we are to Him, the sharper will be our spiritual discernment.

A fuller experience of love for God (v. 9) will result in a finer evaluation of life (v. 10a).

A Fairer Example of Living (1:10b)

Paul then prayed for the Philippians to "be sincere and blameless until the day of Christ." The word "sincere" (*eilikrineis*) has a couple of possible derivations, the most likely of which is "tested by sunshine." When the ancients made porcelain vessels, they often broke or cracked. Whenever that happened, they mended them with wax. Sometimes when a person just looked at a vase, he would not know if it was cracked. The only sure way to know whether the object had been patched was to hold it up to the sunlight. The wax would immediately become visible. When the objects were not patched, that is when they were pure, the merchants would advertise them as being *sine cera*, without wax. From that background comes our word, sincere. To be sincere means to be pure enough to stand the test of sunlight.

Paul also prayed that the Philippians would be "blameless." The word Paul used for *blameless (aproskopoi)* was used to name that part of a trap to which the bait was attached. It was a snare which caused an animal to fall into a trap. To be blameless means not to be a stumbling block or a snare which caused someone else to fall.

In these two words, sincere and blameless, Paul was referring to the inward and the outward parts of our character. As concerns ourself, we are to be pure. As concerns others, we are to be blameless. Paul said to the Philippians, "That is the kind of example I want you to be."

How can we be that kind of example? How can we be inwardly pure and outwardly blameless? The third element of Paul's prayer grows naturally out of the other two. We are able to be pure and blameless (v. 10b) because of our ability to discriminate between the good and the bad, between the better and the best, and give our attention to those things that are excellent (v. 10a). We will be able to discriminate between the good and the bad and give our attention to the things that are excellent (v. 10a) when we experience a deeper love for God (v. 9).

A fuller experience of love (v. 9) will lead to a finer evaluation of life which will result in a fairer example of living (v. 10).

A Further Exaltation of the Lord (1:11)

We hear a great deal in our day about roots. Everyone is trying to discover his roots. More important than our roots is our fruit. God desires each one of us to produce fruit in our lives that will bring glory to Him. We are to magnify God in every part of our lives. That means our hands are to be employed in happy service, our lips are to bear clear testimony, our feet are to be happily running His errands, our knees are to be bent in prayer for His kingdom, and our families are to be reflections of His concern. We are to bear fruit for Christ and thus glorify God. That should be the purpose of every Christian.

How can we do that? How can our lives glorify God? This fourth element of Paul's prayer grows naturally out of the other three. We bring glory to God (v. 11) by exhibiting in our lives the kind of holiness that can be described as sincere and without blame. We exhibit this holiness in our lives by discerning between the different opportunities before us and giving ourselves to that which is best (v. 10). We are able to determine what is best because of our love for God.

A fuller experience of love (v. 9) will lead to a finer evaluation of life which will lead to a fairer example of living (v. 10) which will result in a further exaltation of the Lord (v. 11). Each element of Paul's concern grew out of the other.

Attached to *Poor Richard's Almanac* in 1758 was a little poem that expresses what I am saying: "A little neglect may breed mischief; for want of a nail, the shoe was lost; for want of a shoe the horse was lost; for want of a horse the rider was lost; for want of a rider the war was lost. All for the want of a nail." You start with the nail. If there were no nail, there would be no shoe; no shoe, no horse; no horse, no rider; no rider, no victory. Each was a natural progression from and came out of the other.

So many today are trying to approach the Christian life from the wrong starting point. The starting point of the Christian life is love for God. If there is no love, there will be no sense of what is vital. If there is no sense of what is vital, there will be no pure and blameless life. If there is no pure and blameless life, there will be no glorifying God. It all begins with our love for God. That is why when someone asked Jesus which was the greatest commandment, He began with this: "You shall love the Lord your God with all your heart, and with all your soul, and with all your mind" (Matt. 22:37). There will be no perception and, thus, no purity and, thus, no pleasing God without that.

For Discussion

1. Make a list of the things for which you are most thankful. Share the list with the group.

2. In what ways can you participate in the spread of the gospel today?

3. Name some of the Christians whom you love in the Lord because of their contribution to the kingdom of God.

4. How does our love for God impact our responsibilities and relationships as Christians? Relate to Jesus' statement in Matthew 22:36-40.

5. Why is it difficult to make moral decisions today? What are some resources in making those moral decisions?

3 | The Optimistic Prisoner

Philippians 1:12-20

Viktor Frankl knew the reality of suffering and deprivation as a prisoner of war in World War II. His experience in Nazi German prison camps enabled him to see life at its worst. Some individuals survived the horrors of prison camp while others did not. Frankl wanted to know why. After carefully studying his fellow prisoners, Frankl concluded, "Everything can be taken from men but one thing: the last of human freedoms—to choose one's attitude in any given set of circumstances."[1]

Some are perpetual pessimists like the little boy who was preparing for a test. "I'm going to fail this test," the boy told his dad, "because I don't understand the material." His father responded, "Son, you have to be positive." "OK," the boy replied, "I'm positive I'm going to fail this test!"

Others are incurably optimistic like the ninety-year-old man who married a twenty-four-year-old girl. For the wedding, he bought a new suit with two pairs of pants! Then, he bought a new house on a thirty-year loan next to the elementary school so the children would not have far to walk!

Optimism is a choice! In the most unlikely circumstances, one can still choose to be optimistic. Paul made that choice. Under arrest in Rome with the possibility of death before him, Paul was optimistic. What was the basis for Paul's optimism?

Because It Was Good for the Gospel (1:12-13)

Paul was an optimistic prisoner because he knew his circumstances were good for the gospel.

To what circumstances did Paul refer in verse 12? He could have been referring to the physical abuse he experienced throughout his ministry. A litany of this physical mistreatment is found in 2 Corinthians 11:24-28. More likely, Paul had in mind the recent experiences culminating in his imprisonment. After his arrest by the Jewish leaders, Paul was brought before Felix. He was accused in the presence of Festus. He was hauled in to testify before Agrippa. He was shipwrecked on his way to Rome. He was imprisoned after he arrived in Rome.[2] Things could not have been much worse for the apostle Paul. Suffering was a part of his daily diet. Unpleasant circumstances were an inescapable reality of his life. Yet, Paul did not express gloom over his circumstances but joy.

What was the secret of that optimism? Paul could be optimistic in his suffering because he said "my circumstances have turned out for the greater progress of the gospel" (v. 12). The Philippians were afraid Paul's imprisonment would lead to the curtailment of the gospel. On the contrary, Paul's imprisonment led to a furtherance of the gospel.

The word translated "furtherance" (KJV) or "greater progress" (NASB) is *prokopen*. The word means "to cut before." That word was used of an detachment of woodcutters who preceded the regular army and cut a road through the otherwise impenetrable forest. Thus, the army would be able to advance into areas it could not otherwise have gone. Paul believed the gospel had pushed into some pioneer areas because of his suffering.

Paul gave a specific example of this in verse 13: "My imprisonment in the cause of Christ has become well known throughout the whole praetorian guard." To understand what Paul meant, we need to reconstruct the circumstances of Paul's life. When he arrived in Rome, Paul was imprisoned. He was eventually allowed to have his own hired lodging and was under the care of a soldier who was his guard twenty-four hours a day (Acts 28:16,30). In both Acts 28:20 and Ephesians 6:20, Paul referred to the chains in which he was bound. The Greek word (*halusis*) described a short length of chain by which the wrist of a prisoner was bound to the wrist of a guard. The "praetorian guard" (*praitorion*) was the elite of the Roman Army stationed in Rome, about ten thousand strong, who were the real power of the Roman Empire.

Do you get the picture? Twenty-four hours a day, one after another of these select soldiers was chained to the apostle Paul and forced to be with him. They heard the conversations Paul had with his visitors. They listened to him pray. They watched as he dictated his epistles. They listened as he told them about Jesus. Talk about a captive audience—Paul had it. As Warren Wiersbe put it, "Little did the Romans realize that the chains they affixed to his wrists would release Paul instead of bind him!"[3]

Paul's imprisonment provided the opportunity for the gospel of Christ to penetrate into the ranks of the most powerful men in the world, and from them into the city of Rome. He would have never had that opportunity if he had not been imprisoned.

How can we face our problems with a spirit of optimism? We learn some lessons from Paul.

The Problem Solver Instead of the Problem

Many people are stifled in life today because they see only their problems. Husbands and wives do not enjoy marriage because they see only the problems. Employees do not enjoy their jobs because they always talk about the problems. Young people may not develop their gifts because they think only about the problems. Most people see only the problems, but Paul was different. Paul looked past the problems to the Problem Solver "who is able to do exceeding abundantly beyond all that we ask or think" (Eph. 3:20).

The Opportunity Instead of the Obstacle

Many people use the circumstances of their lives to explain their failure. They say, "My principal had it in for me, and that is why I did not do well in school" or they say, "I was born with a handicap and that is why I have not achieved anything" or they say, "My husband left me and that is why my life is a wreck" or they say, "My boss does not like me and that is why I have not reached my goals." They allow their problems to become obstacles which stop them dead in their tracks, but Paul was different. He saw his problems not as obstacles but as opportunities. Consequently, he took the steps to transform adversity into the advancement of the gospel.

Victory Instead of Defeat

Many people expect to be defeated by life. They are programmed for failure. They begin each day by saying, "I wonder what is going to go wrong today?" A sign on an office wall stated, "When one resigns to fate, his resignation is accepted." Many today have resigned to fate, and their resignation has been accepted, but Paul was different. Because he focused on the Problem Solver instead of the problem, he saw his circumstances as opportunities instead of obstacles. Consequently, he expected victory rather than defeat.

Paul was an optimistic prisoner because his confinement provided an unparalleled opportunity to give a witness for Christ. It was good for the gospel.

Because It Was Good for the Church (1:14-18)

In verse 14, we see another reason for Paul's optimism. He was an optimistic prisoner because he knew his circumstances were good for the church.

Paul explained that "most of the brethren, trusting in the Lord because of my imprisonment, have far more courage to speak the word of God without fear." The word translated "many" in the *King James Version* should actually be "most." The word "brethren" refers to the Christians there in Rome. The word "speak" (*lalein*) does not mean preaching, but it refers to everyday conversation.

Paul's unpleasant circumstances, how he responded to them, and how God's grace was experienced in them were an inspiration to the other Christians in Rome. Before they had been fearful. Now they were boldly sharing Christ in their everyday conversation. His circumstances invoked courage in the Roman Christians.

Remember Paul used the word "most" in verse 14. All of the brethren were not inspired by Paul. Paul elaborated on this in verse 15. Paul divided the Christians in Rome into two categories: those who "are preaching Christ even from envy and strife" and those who are preaching Christ "from good will." Both groups were heralding the gospel. No one was accused of preaching a different gospel as Paul accused some in Galatia (Gal. 1:6), nor were any of them preaching "another Jesus" as Paul accused some at Corinth (2 Cor. 11:4). However, while all of them were proclaiming the true gospel, all of them were not activated by the right motives.

Paul's Friends (1:16)

Paul referred to the good guys in verse 16. (Notice that the NASB translation reverses the order of verses 16 and 17 from the KJV.) He said, "the latter do it out of love, knowing that I am appointed for the defense of the gospel." These Roman Christians had a love for God and for the gospel. They also supported Paul. The word translated "knowing" is a derivative of *oida*, which means to perceive. What did they perceive? They perceived Paul was appointed for the defense of the gospel. The word translated "defense," from which we get our word *apologetic*, is a technical word used in the law courts to speak of the verbal defense presented by a lawyer who defends his client.

These Christians did not begrudge Paul the position God had given to him. They were not envious of the unique gifts God gave to Paul to carry out that assignment. Because they loved God and the gospel, they rejoiced in the marvelous work Paul was doing. They perceived his work was of God.

Paul's Enemies (1:17)

Paul referred to the other group in verse 17: "The former proclaim Christ out of selfish ambition, rather than from pure motives, thinking to cause me distress in my imprisonment." Christians were in Rome before Paul arrived there. The leaders of the Roman church had worked long and hard to establish the church there. They had poured their lives into the church. They had a vested interest in the church. They were the ones looked up to and respected and called on. But when Paul came, all the attention was directed toward him. Christians began to murmur, "Paul said this," and "Paul said that." Pagans in the street discussed this strange prisoner who boldly shared a new message about God. Paul was getting all the attention, and the other preachers could not stand it.

Because these Christian leaders were losing their hold on the Roman church, they started working harder in order to strengthen their positions of leadership. Their motive was not love for God, but jealousy of the apostle Paul. They did not want to exalt Christ; they wanted to exalt themselves. Their ultimate desire was not to make Christ's name known but to make Paul miserable.

Paul's Response (1:18)

How did Paul respond to these who were preaching the gospel out of envy and who were trying to make him more miserable? Paul rejoiced in what was happening (v. 18). He rejoiced in those who were proclaiming the gospel out of love and pure motives. And he rejoiced in those who were proclaiming the gospel out of envy and impure motives. Why? Because he said, "Only that in every way, whether in pretense or in truth, Christ is proclaimed" (v. 18).

Do you get the picture? Now, instead of just one person sharing Christ, Christians all over Rome were sharing Christ, not just in preaching, but in their everyday conversation. Because of that, Paul rejoiced!

God will really begin to bless our churches when we rejoice in the work others are doing for Him, even when they do things different from us and even with a different motive from us.

Paul was an optimistic prisoner because his circumstances allowed the work of the church to be strengthened. It was good for the church.

Because It Was Good for Paul (1:19)

Paul was also an optimistic prisoner because his circumstances were also good for him.

Paul said, "For I know that this shall turn out for my deliverance." The word translated "deliverance" is actually the word "salvation" (*soterian*). Paul said his imprisonment would turn out for his salvation. What did Paul mean?

The word "salvation" in verse 19 did not mean personal safety. Paul was not saying, "I know I will be released from prison and be safe," for in verse 21, he said it made no difference whether he lived or died. Nor did it mean salvation in the sense of eternal security with God. We are saved not by what we endure but by what Christ endured, not because of our suffering, but because of His.

What did Paul mean? The word "salvation" in verse 19 meant "personal well being." God was going to work in Paul's suffering to mold him into a better person. That is why he could be an optimistic prisoner, because this imprisonment was an instrument God would use to make him better.

So often we cry when suffering comes. We strike out at God when the circumstances of our lives are unpleasant. Something happens and we moan, "Why me?" and wallow in our self-pity. But the lesson history has taught us is that great souls graduate from the school of conflict, never from the school of convenience. When there is no calamity, there is no courage; no hardship, no hardiness; no stress, no strength; no suffering, no sympathy; no cross, no crown!

Richard Baxter (1615-1691), who lived in seventeenth-century England, was one of history's most memorable preachers. But throughout his life, he was plagued by one illness after another. For years, he entered the pulpit in the fear that he might not leave it alive. His biographer pointed to his illness as the source of his greatness, for it weakened temptation, kept him from valuing the world too highly, and taught him the importance of every moment of time.

John Bunyan (1628-1688), another English divine of the seventeenth century, spent twelve years in prison. He later referred to his prison as a hill from which he could see great things.

What is your handicap? What is your unpleasant circumstance? What is it that binds your life? What causes you to suffer? Don't bemoan these things. Rejoice in them! God can use them to mold you into the person He wants you to be.

Every experience of suffering is a great crossroads in our lives. We can respond in anger and become bitter. Or, we can accept suffering as the chisel God uses to sculpt marred sinners into saints.

Paul's imprisonment was going to be an instrument which God used for his own well-being. Notice the two factors by which this glorious result would be obtained.

The Prayer of the Christians (1:19)

Paul mentioned first the prayer of the people. God's power is available and adequate to meet every need of our life, to come into every circumstance of our life and make something good out of it. It is the prayer of God's people, our intercession one for another, that releases that power and sets it to work. The command to pray for one another is not just a magnificent privilege. It is also an awesome responsibility.

We see the practice and power of prayer repeatedly in the New Testament church. Paul wrote to the Thessalonians: "Brethren, pray for us" (1 Thess. 5:25). Paul commended the Corinthians because "you also joining in helping us through your prayers, that thanks may be given by many persons on our behalf for the favor bestowed upon us through the prayers of many" (2 Cor. 1:11). Before he came to the Romans, he asked their prayer (Rom. 15:30-32). When he left the Ephesians, he prayed for them (Acts 20:36). Prayer was the perpetual pattern of the first Christians.

The Power of the Spirit (1:19)

Prayer was an effective tool for accomplishing the mission of the church because prayer unleashed the power of the Spirit. In addition to the prayers of the Philippians, Paul mentioned "the provision of the Spirit of Jesus Christ."

Human intercession and divine intervention! We sometimes hesitate to put those two ideas side by side. Yet, here they are, cited by Paul as the two factors which would see him through: the prayers of the people and the power of God's Spirit.

Write down the names of five people who are going through a difficult time, who are being beset by unpleasant circumstances. Then, begin to intercede to the Father on behalf of those people every day. Then, they will be able to say about you what Paul said about his Christian brothers in Rome, "This thing has turned out for my well-being through your prayers and the provision of the spirit of Jesus Christ."

For Discussion

1. Why do people suffer?
2. Since our attitude determines how we view our circumstances, how can we develop a more positive attitude?
3. Which is more important, our message or our motive? How did Paul respond to the different motives of the Roman Christians?
4. What difficulty or problem in your life has God used to develop you?
5. How does prayer help us deal with difficult situations?

4 | When There's No Way to Lose

Philippians 1:21-26

During a heated debate at a church conference, one of the members stood up and delivered a tirade against universities and education, suggesting no money in the budget be sent to support institutions of higher learning. He concluded his diatribe with a declaration that he was thankful he had never been corrupted by any contact with a college. The moderator responded, "Do I understand that you thank God for your ignorance?" The disgruntled member replied, "Well, yes, if you want to put it that way." The moderator concluded, "All I have to say is that you have a great deal to be thankful for."

Ignorance abounds in our world. The antidote to ignorance is education. William Barclay, gifted biblical scholar, said in his autobiography that every person needs two educations. He needs to be taught how to make a living, and then, he needs to be taught how to live.[1]

Paul knew how to make a living, for he supported himself through most of his ministry with his tent making in order not to be a burden to the churches. He was the first in a long history of bivocational ministers. He knew how to make a living. Even more important, Paul knew how to live. We see the secret of Paul's life in our text.

Paul's Purpose (1:20)

What was Paul's purpose in life? What was his ambition? Paul said he wanted to live so that "Christ shall even now, as always be exalted in my body, whether by life or by death."

Paul's purpose was not to be successful. Therefore, he was not bothered by an occasional failure. His purpose was not to be popular. So he was not disturbed when others did not like him. His purpose was not to be comfortable. Unpleasant circumstances did not throw him. Paul's purpose was not even to have a long life. Even death did not frighten him. Paul's purpose was to exalt Christ.

The Greek word translated "exalt" (*megalunthesetai*) means "to make great" or "to make conspicuous." Whatever he did, Paul wanted to make Christ conspicuous, to make Christ look great. He wanted to magnify Christ in everything he did. That was Paul's purpose.

Why does Christ need to be magnified? Because, like the stars in the sky, Jesus Christ seems to be very far away to some people. As a telescope magnifies the stars and brings them closer, so we are to magnify Christ and bring Him closer to life through our faith.

Why does Christ need to be magnified? Because, like some cells which are so tiny they cannot be seen with the naked eye, Jesus seems to be very small to some people. As a microscope magnifies these tiny cells and makes them visible, so we are to magnify Christ and make Him visible through our faith.

Warren Wiersbe says magnifying Christ means being a "lens" that makes a "little Christ look very big and a distant Christ look very close."[2]

That's what Paul did. He was a lens which magnified Christ to those around him. That was the secret of Paul's inimitable achievement for Christ. That is why, 2,000 years later, we are still talking about Paul. That is the explanation of the comment made by a preacher of this generation who said: "Everywhere Paul went there was a revolution; everywhere I go there is a tea party." We will never understand Paul or other Christians through the centuries who have made significant achievement for Christ without realizing that behind their achievement was this simple yet unswerving purpose: to exalt Christ in everything they did.

How Can We Exalt Christ?

By keeping pure.—Paul told the Philippians his eager expectation was that Christ would be honored in his body (Phil. 1:20). After Paul explained how immorality perverted the purpose for which God gave us our bodies, Paul concluded, "Glorify God in your body" (1 Cor. 6:20). When we remain pure in the midst of an immoral world, others watching us will be forced to admit Christ makes a difference in our lives. Therefore, Christ will be exalted.

By producing fruit.—At the beginning of His ministry, Jesus told the disciples in the Sermon on the Mount, "Let your light shine before men in such a way that they may see your good works, and glorify your Father who is in heaven" (Matt. 5:16). At the end of His ministry, Jesus said to the disciples in the upper room, "By this is My Father glorified, that you bear much fruit, and so prove to be My disciples" (John 15:8). When we commit ourselves to spiritual concerns in a world motivated by financial concerns, others watching us will realize Christ makes a difference in our lives. Therefore, Christ will be exalted.

By standing firm.—One of the most remarkable verses in the New Testament is Matthew 27:54. For three years Jesus had been doing His mighty works. He had been presenting His matchless teachings. He had been making His marvelous provisions. None of that impressed the Roman soldiers. Without another thought, they nailed Jesus to the cross and began to throw dice to see who would cop His garment. But Matthew 27:54 says that as Jesus hung on the cross, one of the soldiers said, "Truly this was the Son of God!" What made the difference. The way Jesus lived did not impress the soldiers. What impressed them was the way Jesus died. When they saw the light of faith which persisted even in the darkness of the cross, that impressed them. When we stand firm in our faith in the midst of difficult times when so many people fall apart, others watching us will realize Christ makes a difference in our lives. Therefore, Christ will be exalted.

Paul's Philosophy (1:21*a*)

Paul's purpose was to exalt Christ (v. 20). Out of this purpose Paul developed a philosophy of life. We see it in the first part of verse 21. Paul's philosophy was this: "For to me, to live is Christ, and to die is gain." All the rest of our text is an elaboration of this central statement in verse 21. As Paul considered his future (and remember he was under house arrest with the possibility of imprisonment and even death ahead), he saw two possibilities looming before him. He could live or he could die. Whichever happened, Paul was convinced he could not lose.

What if Paul lived? What then? Paul declared, "For to me, to live is Christ." Paul's thought becomes clear if we write down the word life, then put an $=$, and then write down the word *Christ*. Life $=$ Christ. Or we can express the equation in a negative way. If Christ were to be taken out of Paul's life, nothing would be left. Life - Christ = zero. That was the mathematical equation of Paul's life: Life = Christ.

What Did Paul Mean by That Equation?

The initiator of his life.—To say life = Christ meant Jesus was the initiator of Paul's life. Life for Paul, real life with a capital "L," did not begin when he was born a Roman citizen, when he graduated from the school of Gamaliel, or when he became a Pharisee. It began with Christ. Paul began to live only when He came to know Jesus.

The ideal of his life.—To say life = Christ meant Jesus was the ideal of Paul's life. Jesus was the goal toward which Paul moved. Paul did not live for himself. He lived for Christ. He did not serve himself. He served Christ. Every person fits either into Philippians 1:21 or Philippians 2:21. Philippians 1:21 says, "For me to live is Christ." Philippians 2:21 says, "They all seek after their own interests, not those of Christ Jesus." Where do you fit? What are you living for? There was no question about where Paul fit. Life not only began with Christ. It also existed for Christ. Christ was his ideal.

The inspiration of his life.—To say life = Christ meant Jesus was the inspiration of Paul's life. Webster defines inspiration as a "stimulus to creative thought or action."[3] That's what Christ was to Paul. Paul said, "Jesus lives in me, and He gives me the stimulus, the motivation, the power to press on toward the goal. He is my inspiration."

Living was a glorious experience for Paul because Jesus Christ was the initiator of life, the ideal toward which he strived, and the inspiration which made it possible. That's why Paul said, "For to me, to live is Christ." Paul knew no life apart from Christ.

Paul's Prospects (1:21*b*)

In the last part of verse 21, Paul talked about his prospects. Paul said, "For to me, to live is Christ." However, Paul might not live. Instead, he might die. What then? Paul said, "In that case, to die is gain." The word gain (*kerdos*) is an old word for any gain or profit made on an investment. We might translate that Greek word *dividend.* Paul said, "If I die, I will cash in all of my investments and will receive both principal and interest so I will have more of Christ even than when I was living!"

Paul was in a no-lose situation. Whatever happened to him, he was going to be OK. He was in a situation where there was no way to lose. That is the prospect for every person who is in Christ Jesus.

What Did Paul Hope to Gain by Death?

Relief.—Paul feared one thing more than anything else. He was not afraid to die, nor did he hesitate in the face of opposition. Criticism did not cause him to tremble nor did misunderstanding by others. What did Paul fear? He feared living so long he would no longer be effective in his service for the Lord (1 Cor. 9:27). Death was gain because it would relieve him of that possibility.

Release.—Death was also gain because it would bring release from the troubles and pain which came from his constant imprisonment and continuous mental and physical abuse.

Richard Baxter, whom I have already mentioned, was a gifted preacher. However, he suffered much physical pain during the closing years of his life. He took unpopular stands and consequently spent years in prison. On his deathbed, a friend came by to comfort him. When he asked Richard how he was doing, the great preacher responded, "Friend, I am almost well!"[4]

Paul would echo that testimony. Death was gain because it would release him from the limitations and difficulties of his physical body.

Realization.—Death was a door which led into the presence of Christ where Paul could attain what he most desired: the full knowledge of Christ (Phil. 3:10-14). Death was not less of life but more of life. It was not an end but a new beginning. It was not the period at the conclusion of life but a comma which punctuated life with a new significance.

That is what it is like to serve Christ. We invest our life, our energy, our gifts, and our resources. Then we experience the power, protection, and provisions of God. As we look at our life in Christ, we say, "It doesn't get any better than this." Then when we die we discover it does get better than this, for we will experience more of Christ's power, more of Christ's protection, more of Christ's provisions than we ever experienced in life. For every Christian, as for Paul, to die is gain because it enables us to realize the fullness of the promises and provisions of Christ.

When Paul considered the relief, release, and realization death would bring, he made this bold declaration, "For me, to die is gain!"

Paul's Perplexity (1:22-24)

When Paul considered his prospects for the future, he became somewhat perplexed about which would be better: life or death. We see his perplexity in verses 22-26. Because both life and death offered the possibility of pursuing his purpose, Paul said in verse 22. "I do not know which to choose," and in verse 23, "I am hard pressed from both directions." Paul used a word which described a traveler going through a narrow passageway, with a wall of rock on either side, unable to go to the side but only able to go forward. Paul could not avoid the future with its options of either life or death. Paul used two words to describe these two options. The possibility of dying and being with the Lord he described as "very much better" (v. 23). The possibility of living and serving the Lord on this earth he described as "more necessary" (v. 24).

The Cessation of Life (v. 23)

Paul used a triple comparative to describe the option of dying. The English translation "very much better" picks up a little of that emphasis. It is not only much better, it is very much better. Why is this option "very much better"? Because at death Paul would be in the very presence of Christ. Although death is often accompanied by the pain of illness and the pain of parting, for the Christian, death should not be a terror, because death is the passageway through which we go into the eternal presence of Christ.

Tony Campolo tells of a funeral service at Mount Carmel Baptist Church in West Philadelphia. The service for the twenty-year-old man was marked by grief. The pastor, for the first fifteen minutes of the service, pronounced the promises of a resurrection. He walked down to the family and spoke words of comfort to them. He then did an unusual thing. He turned to the open casket and began to address the deceased. He thanked him for his life and his faith. When he had finished this litany of memories, he said, "That's all I have to say except this: Good night, Clarence, Good night!" He slammed the lid on the casket, turned to the congregation with a smile on his face and declared, "But I know God is going to give Clarence a good morning!" With that, the choir started singing, "On that great gettin' up morning we shall rise, we shall rise!"[5] In that rather shocking way, the preacher declared and demonstrated the biblical truth sounded by the psalmist: "Weeping may last for the night, But a shout of joy comes in the morning" (Ps. 30:5).

The Continuation of Life (v. 24)

Paul used a double comparative to describe the option of living. He said it is "more necessary" to "remain on in the flesh" (v. 24). The Greek word translated "more necessary" is the same word Paul used in 1 Corinthians 9:16 when he said, "I am under compulsion; for woe is me if I do not preach the gospel." It speaks of divine constraint, an inescapable incentive.

Wilfred Grenfell (1865-1940), medical missionary to Labrador, spoke of his work wherever he went. One night in a meeting, he described his early years in Labrador, revealing something of his hardship and struggle. Afterwards, a woman praised him for his sacrifice with a note of reverence mixed with pity. Grenfell responded, "Oh, you don't understand. I was having the time of my life!" Likewise, longer life for Paul would simply provide more opportunities for the joy of Christian service.

The thought of dying did not frighten Paul because at death he would be ushered into the presence of Christ, and that would be glory. Even though the thought of dying was appealing, Paul kept living and serving God in his life because he was under divine constraint to do so. Because of Paul's philosophy of life, he could face either death or life with equal joy. If he died, he would be able to experience Christ's presence. If he lived, he would be able to fulfill Christ's purpose. Either way, he won.

Paul's Product (1:25-26)

When Paul thought about his prospects, he was convinced God would allow him to live longer to carry out his ministry among the Philippians. This was not a prophetic inspiration but a personal conviction. His compulsion to minister to the Philippians convinced him his ministry was not yet over. His ministry would lead to two results.

Progress (v. 25)

The word "progress" (v. 25) is the same word used in verse 12. The word referred to woodcutters who blazed new trails for the army, cutting away the underbrush. Paul told the Philippians they would experience things they had never experienced before through his ministry.

The spirit of Paul was that of an explorer who said, "I will not follow where the path may lead, but I will go where there is no path, and I will leave a trail." Paul left a trail which not only the Christians in Philippi but also Christians of the ages have followed.

Joy (v. 25)

The word "joy" is the Greek word *charan*. The kind of joy Paul had in mind was not just an emotional mood. It is a characteristic of life that grows out of our relationship with the Lord. Paul told the Philippians they would experience a deep, abiding joy like nothing the world offers through his ministry.

Robert Fowler was captain of the sailing vessel *Woodhouse* which left England for America in the late 1600s. The ship docked in England for repairs, which took several days. The Quakers left the ship and infiltrated the surrounding community with the Christian message. Robert Fowler put this summary statement in the log, "The Ministers of Christ were not idle, they gathered sticks, kindled a fire, and left it burning." What a beautiful description of the life of Paul. Everywhere he went he left a fire of joy and faith burning behind him.

What a thought! Paul's purpose in life was to exalt Christ. When he pursued that purpose, it produced confidence within him so he could face any circumstances that came. And it produced growth and joy in others.

For Discussion

1. How can we glorify Christ in our lives?
2. Fill in the blank: "For me to live is _____." Discuss some of the different philosophies in the world today.
3. Why do people fear death so much?
4. What does the Bible teach about death?
5. In what ways can we produce progress and joy in the lives of others?

5 | Living Like a Christian

Philippians 1:27-30

Philip Yancey, a well-known Christian writer, categorizes Christians into two sets: Christian entertainers and Christian servants. The Christian entertainers, Yancey says, are those musicians, actors, writers, speakers, and comedians who fill our periodicals, dominate our seminars, and appear on our television screens. They have fame, prestige, and money. The Christian servants, on the other hand, are rarely in the spotlight. They toil unnoticed in remote places. They live among the rejects of society and work for low pay, long hours, and no applause. Their talents and skills are given to the poor and uneducated. Yet somehow, in the process of losing their lives, they have found them and attained rewards that the famous never experience.[1]

This categorization of Christians into two groups, Christian entertainers and Christian servants, raises an interesting question. What does it really mean to live like a Christian? Are we to be entertainers or servants? Paul gave some answers to that question in our text.

The *King James Version*, "Only let your conversation be as it becometh the gospel of Christ" (v. 27) misses the meaning of Paul's statement. The Greek word translated "conversation" in the *King James Version* is *politeuesthe* which is the word from which our word *politics* comes. It derives from the Greek word *polis* which means city. Literally, the word means *citizenship.* It refers not to our conversation but to our conduct. The meaning of the word goes even deeper than that. The word *politeuesthe* does not refer just to our conduct. It refers to conduct which is our duty because we are members of a certain group.

As Christians, we are citizens in the kingdom of God. As citizens in God's kingdom, we have a certain duty to the group.

What is our duty? What is our obligation as members of the kingdom of God? Paul declared: "Only conduct yourselves in a manner worthy of the gospel of Christ" (v. 27). Paul painted an interesting picture here. The words translated "worthy of" actually mean of equal weight to. The words refer to a set of scales. Picture an ancient scale with a crossbar and a little cup hanging from each end of the crossbar. On one side of the scale is the gospel and all it stands for. On the other side of the scale is our life. Our life—the way we live, the way we conduct ourselves—should be of equal weight to the expectations of the gospel. That is our duty as Christians.

What does it mean to conduct our lives in a manner worthy of the gospel? Notice four answers Paul gave to that question.

Live with Tenacity (1:27)

Paul told the Philippians they were living like Christians when they were "standing firm in one spirit." The word translated "standing firm" is the Greek word *stekete.* The word means tenacity or perseverance.

A 104-year-old man was being interviewed by a newspaper reporter. "How did you do it?" the reporter asked. The centenarian answered, "I ate the right food, got plenty of sleep each night, didn't fool around, and never indulged in alcohol, smokes, or chewin'." The reporter replied, "I had an uncle like that but he died at fifty-five. Can you explain that?" "Sure," the old man replied, "he just didn't keep it up long enough."

What is most important about our Christian life is not what we do but how long we do it. The failure in most Christian lives comes, not because we don't do the right things, but because we don't keep them up long enough. Being a Christian does not just mean serving Christ when you are a young man or young woman. It means serving Christ all your life. Being a Christian does not just mean doing good when the going is easy. It means doing good whether the going is easy or not. Standing firm means perseverance and tenacity for the cause of Christ.

How can we have tenacity? Paul said we are to stand firm "in one spirit." Members of the church should be fused together. In other words, we do not have to stand firm alone. In fact, we cannot stand firm alone. We stand firm for the Lord only because we stand in a unity of spirit with other Christians. That is why identifying with a church, joining a church, and getting involved in a church are so important. We cannot stand alone as Christians. We can stand only as we identify ourselves with and unite with other Christians in the fellowship of the church.

When Criticism Comes

We are to stand firm when criticism comes. Have you ever heard of Charles Simeon? Probably not, for he was born over 200 years ago. While a student at Cambridge University in England, he was preparing for the ministry. One day he walked past the Holy Trinity Church in the heart of the university campus. He said to himself, *What a thrill it would be if God would call me to this church where I can preach the gospel in the midst of this university campus.* In 1782 God answered his prayer and he became the church's pastor. However, at first he was confronted with the most violent opposition. The seat holders in the congregation boycotted the services and locked the doors to their pews. As a result, for more than ten years, the congregation had to stand up during the entire worship service. Simeon persevered and gradually won the respect of the congregational leaders. For fifty-five years he was pastor of Holy Trinity Church, systematically proclaiming the message of God's Word. Why? Because he stood firm when criticism came.

Think about your life. Is someone critical of you? Do you have someone who is bothering you? Does someone not like you? What do you do when criticism comes? Paul said, "Don't give up. Stand firm."

When Failure Comes

We are to stand firm when failure comes. A little boy asked his dad to come outside and watch him hit the ball. The boy tossed up the ball, swung the bat, and missed. "Strike one," the boy said. He tried it again with the same result. "Strike two," he mumbled. He threw the ball up again and missed it a third time. "Strike three," he said. Then he looked at his dad and said, "Man, I'm some kind of pitcher, aren't I!"

What do you do when you strike out in life? What do you do when you have failed? Paul said, "Don't give up. Stand firm."

When Disaster Comes

We are to stand firm when disaster comes. The name Lee Iacocca has become a household word in America, but he did not get where he is without difficulties. After thirty-two years with the Ford Motor Company and after eight years as president of Ford, Lee Iacocca was fired. At the age of fifty-four he went to his new office in a warehouse, far removed from the luxury of his executive suite at Ford. That could have been the end of Lee Iacocca, but it wasn't. Today, we know him as the man who turned Chrysler around and made it one of our century's greatest success stories. Why? Because he stood firm when disaster came.

What do you do when disaster comes? How do you handle unexpected, undeserved setbacks? Paul said, "Don't give up. Stand firm."

Live with Harmony (1:27)

Paul also told the Philippians they were living like Christians when they were "with one mind striving together for the faith of the gospel." The Greek word (*sunathlountes*) means striving together. It is a word from the field of athletics and literally means to wrestle together or to wrestle in harmony. A comparable picture today is eleven men on a football team working together to move the ball toward the goal line. It is an active word. The emphasis, however, is not on the activity but on the harmony in which the activity is carried out.

The Christian life is one of activity, a life of commitment. We are not just to stand firm. We are not just to hold our ground. We are to move out on the attack. We are to take the offensive. However, as we do, we are to work in harmony with other Christians. We are to work as a team.

In the church today we have become so judgmental of each other that we have almost destroyed our harmony. When we judge other Christians, it is not usually because they are bad but because they are different.

How we need to realize today that God made us all different. And God needs all of us preachers and all of our churches, as different as we are from one another, to learn how to strive together in harmony for the faith of Jesus Christ. We are most like Christ and therefore living most like Christians not when we scrutinize others to see if they are as Christian as we are but when we recognize that we are all part of the body of Christ and strive together with one mind for the faith of the Gospel.

Several years ago Jimmy Durante was asked to be part of a show for some World War II veterans. Although his schedule was busy, he did agree to do a short monologue after which he would have to leave immediately for his next appointment. When Jimmy went on stage that night, he finished his short monologue and then started another. The applause grew louder and louder as he did monologue after monologue. Finally, after a long time, he took his last bow and left the stage. Someone stopped him backstage and said, "I thought you had to go after a few minutes. What happened?" Durante answered, "I did have to go, but I can show you the reason I stayed." He pointed to the front row where two men were seated next to each other, each of whom had lost an arm in the war. One had lost his right arm and the other had lost his left. Together, they were able to clap, and that's exactly what they were doing, loudly and cheerfully.[2]

What a picture for the church today to emulate! What an illustration of Paul's declaration in our text! When we strive together as Christians, each using our unique gifts and resources and personalities and approaches, we accomplish things together for the kingdom of God we could never accomplish alone.

Live with Courage (1:28)

Paul pointed out a third characteristic of Christian living: courage. Paul told the Philippians they were to be "in no way alarmed by your opponents." The word translated "alarmed" is the Greek word *pturomenoi*. The word pictures a horse which is suddenly frightened by an unexpected object. The word means not to be startled or terrified.

Many opponents will rise up against us as we seek to live our Christian lives. It may be someone at school who makes fun of us. It may be someone at work who taunts us because we are a Christian. It may be a member of our family who makes life difficult for us. All of us have adversaries. As Christians, we are to confront them with courage, not fear.

Facing our opponents with courage points to two significant truths.

Our Prospects

A Christian who courageously faces opposition is a living testimony to the world of the ultimate outcome of things. At times, the wicked seem to prosper and the righteous seem to suffer. The psalmist dealt with that reality (Ps. 73) as we do today. The psalmist was perplexed by the prosperity of the wicked. The wicked seemed to be carefree and confident, apparently blessed with a life of abundance (vv. 4-12). On the other hand, the psalmist was confronted by misunderstanding and disaster, leaving him confused and uncertain about life (vv.13-16). When he went to the temple, he understood that the prosperity of the wicked was temporary (vv. 17-20). On the other hand, the temporary difficulties of the righteous would be replaced by eternal glory (vv. 23-26). This awareness produced a new confidence in the psalmist as he faced the world (v. 28).

Like the psalmist, the Christian knows the ultimate outcome of things. Thus, he faces the enemies and inequities of life with confidence and courage. The confidence of the Christian is a revelation to the world that Christ will ultimately prevail.

Our Protection

This confidence, however, is not self-confidence but God-confidence. Paul said that our deliverances are "from God." And God's provisions are always more adequate than our own provisions.

A little boy went with his father into town to buy some supplies. In the store, the boy stood quietly as the father picked up all the things he needed. As they left, the proprietor said to the boy, "Son, you have been so good. Why don't you reach your hand into the candy jar and get a handful of candy?" The little boy said nothing but just stood there. Finally, the proprietor reached his hand into the jar and gave a handful of candy to the boy. On the way home, the father asked his son, "Why didn't you reach into the jar and get the candy yourself? I've never known you to be shy." The boy replied, "I wasn't shy. I just knew his hand was bigger than my hand!" God's hand is always bigger than our hand. When we courageously stand up for Him, His provisions will be more than adequate.

When we live with courage, Paul said, it is a sign or proof to both Christians and non-Christians alike that our adversaries are on the road to destruction and we are on the road to salvation.

Live with Submission (1:29-30)

A Christian also displays submission. Paul said, "For to you it has been granted for Christ's sake, not only to believe in Him, but also to suffer for His sake" (v. 29). The Philippians had heard of Paul's suffering in Rome and earlier in his travels. Paul said, "What has happened to me will also happen to you. Suffering is a part of the Christian life."

How can we evaluate suffering? Paul suggested that suffering "has been granted for Christ's sake." The *King James Version* expresses the idea more clearly with the translation: "For unto you it is given." The word "given" is the same word used to describe the gift of salvation to us. As God gives us the gift of salvation, He also gives us the gift of suffering.

Do you understand what this means? Suffering is one of God's gifts to His children and submitting to this suffering is one of the duties of the Christian. Suffering is not God's goof. Sometimes it is His gift!

What a different view of suffering from the way we normally view it. We usually think of suffering as something which will destroy us and we beg God to take it away. In many cases, that suffering may be a gift from God which He will use to develop us if we will be submissive to Him. We don't need to pray to lose it. We need to pray that God will use it.

Paul Powell tells of a woman named Eloise who was a member of a church which he once pastored. He went back to conduct a funeral at that church. At the graveside, he learned Eloise had just been diagnosed with cancer. Several years earlier she had gone through a cancer operation and a series of treatments and had been pronounced cured. Now, the cancer was back. As she entered the hospital for tests, she was greatly distressed. She was so worried that she could not sleep. She prayed and prayed and prayed until she could pray no more. Finally, she said, "Oh, God, whatever Your will is, I accept it." At that point she told Paul Powell, she experienced a peace she had never experienced before in her life. When the tests came back, her worst fears were confirmed. The cancer was in the advanced stage, and she would probably die soon. But Eloise gave this testimony: "The peace was still there. I wasn't troubled. I wasn't upset. I wasn't worried. When my friends came to visit me and saw how I was responding to this emotionally, they said, 'Eloise, we don't understand.'" "You know, Paul," she added, "I don't understand it either. I think this must be the 'peace that passeth understanding.'"[3]

Have you ever experienced that "peace which passeth understanding" in the midst of your suffering? You can, if you will understand that suffering is not God's goof but God's gift, and if you will submit to Him and His will for your life.

When we submit to life's experiences and allow God to use them to develop us into what He wants us to be, then we are living like a Christian.

Conclusion

How can we live like a Christian? Here are four specific tests to apply to our lives to see if we are living like Christians.

Are we living with tenacity? Do we give up easily, or do we faithfully, day in and day out, continue in our life of commitment and obedience?

Are we living with harmony? Do we create division and conflict everywhere we go, or are we an instrument of God's peace?

Are we living with courage? Do we hesitate when the going gets tough, or are we willing to risk for Christ?

Are we living with submission? Do we rise up and shake our fist at God when things go wrong? Or do we hold on to see what God can do with that suffering?

The incomparable conqueror Alexander the Great heard of a man in his army, also named Alexander, who had turned away from the battle. Alexander the Great called this young man into his presence. "Young man," he said, "Is it true that your name is Alexander?" "Yes," the timid young man responded. "And is it true that you turned and ran instead of fighting in the battle?" "Yes," the man said, "That is true." Alexander the Great replied, "Then, young man, you need either to change your name or change your actions." I wonder if Christ wants to say that to us?

For Discussion

1. Which role best describes the Christian life: Christian entertainers or Christian servants?

2. What can we learn from criticism and failure?

3. What are some specific things we can do to produce harmony in the body of Christ?

4. What creates the greatest fear in your life? What can you do about it?

5. Discuss some difficult experiences in your life and how you made it through them.

6 | Learning How to Get Along

Philippians 2:1-5

In April of 1975, a church in a community some forty miles east of Dallas was split over the issue of speaking in tongues and the gifts of the Spirit. One group had become involved in the charismatic movement and members of the group spoke in tongues. The other group called "The Faithful 86" disagreed vehemently with that experience in the Christian life. The result was a battle royal between the two sides. Holy Week services were interrupted by a fist fight between members. One group changed the locks on the church and then the other group did the same. One group put an advertisement in the paper declaring they were the real First Baptist Church, and then the other group did the same. Finally, under the watchful eye of the city authorities, a vote was taken over whether or not to dismiss the pastor, with one group aligning with him and the other against him.

That tragedy is repeated almost every week in some church at some location: Christians who have been brought together into a fellowship of believers who then experience a rift in that fellowship. Paul saw signs in the church at Philippi of such a possibility, so in the first few verses of the second chapter, Paul sent an urgent admonition to them to maintain their unity.

Two factors can be threats to the unity of the church: false teaching from without and disagreeing members from within. The underlying implication of chapter 1 is that the Philippian Christians stood up well against the heretical teaching from without. However, they were not doing so well with their disagreeing members within. These intramural squabbles threatened to destroy the church, so Paul sent an urgent appeal for them to learn how to get along with their brothers and sisters in Christ.

What Christ Provides (2:1)

Paul began his discussion with a reminder of what Christ provides. Verse 1 contains four clauses, each of which begins with the word "if": "if therefore there is any encouragement in Christ"; "if there is any consolation of love"; "if there is any fellowship of the Spirit"; "if any affection and compassion." In the Greek, the tense and form used assumes these conditions to be true. Thus, we can translate the first phrase, "If therefore there is encouragement in Christ, and you know there is." Or we can substitute the word "since," for the word "if" and translate the phrase, "since there is encouragement in Christ."

These four clauses are statements of fact which are the foundation of the appeal which followed. Because these four things are true, Paul said to the Philippians, in view of these four facts, you ought to get along with each other. These are the motivations for Christian unity.

The Life in Christ

Paul referred first to the "encouragement in Christ." The Greek word translated "encouragement" (*paraklesis*), actually means one who stands by us to encourage us. It is the same word Jesus used in John 14—16 to speak of the Holy Spirit. What is it that comes alongside of us to help us? Paul pointed to the experiences we have "in Christ."

Paul used that unique expression "in Christ" to describe all our connections with and experiences in Jesus Christ: His love for the unlovely, His tendency to look for the best in others, His desire to help people, as well as His willingness to die vicariously for the sins of the world. All of these things we experience in our relationship with Christ should encourage us to get along with one another.

The Love of God

Another motivation is "the consolation of love." The Greek word translated "consolation" (*paramuthion*) is an active word which refers to the tender persuasiveness of love. Paul had in mind the love God has for us. We should be stimulated to Christian unity, we should be motivated to get along with each other, because of the love God has for us.

John expressed the same idea in his epistle when he said, "Beloved, if God so loved us, we also ought to love one another" (1 John 4:11).

The Linking of Our Lives

Paul referred also to "the fellowship of the Spirit." The word translated "fellowship" (*koinonia*) is one of the richest words in the New Testament. It is a word used to refer to the fellowship of believers in the church. The word can also mean "participation." That is the meaning of the word here. Paul was referring to our participation with or our partnership with the Holy Spirit.

The Holy Spirit is the unifying Person in the local church (1 Cor. 12:4-11). The desire of the Holy Spirit is to build up and edify and strengthen the church. We should be stimulated to Christian unity, we should be motivated to get along with each other by our partnership in life with the Holy Spirit.

The Longings of the Heart

Finally, Paul referred to "affection and compassion." The Greek words which the *King James Version* translates as "bowels and mercies" are the words *splagchna* and *oiktirmoi*. The first word *(splagchna)* refers to the seat of compassion. The second word (*oiktirmoi*) refers to the compassion itself. Paul was talking about the virtue of human compassion which comes from within man. Because of our common humanity, something within us responds when we see a person being hurt. Something within us causes us to have compassion for another human. Sometimes, we quench this compassion. Sometimes, we refuse to let it move us to action. It is nevertheless there. Every person, at his best, has a compassion which responds to the hurt of another person.

We should be stimulated to unity, we should be motivated to get along with each other, because of the compassion of the human heart.

Nothing would make Paul's joy any more full than to see the Philippians getting along with each other. Why should they do it? Paul cited four motivations: the life of Christ, the love of God, the linking of their lives together in the fellowship of the church, and the longings of the human heart.

What Christ Demands (2:2-4)

In verse 2 Paul moved from the motivation to the directive itself. In verses 2-4 Paul gave the Christians at Philippi three directives on how to get along.

A Call to Harmony (v. 2)

Paul called on the Philippians to be "of the same mind, maintaining the same love, united in spirit, intent on one purpose." The demand in verse 2 is a call to harmony. Paul offered phrase after phrase which point to the oneness which ought to mold us together in Christ.

He said that we are to be of one mind.—The Greek word (*phronete*) refers to man's thinking capacity. To be of the same mind means to have an identity of ideas, to have minds which are in perfect intellectual harmony like two clocks striking at the very same moment. Paul repeated this idea, in stronger language, in the final phrase of the verse which is translated "intent on one purpose." It is the same Greek word and should be translated "the one thing minding." We are to be of one mind.

He said we are to be of one love.—We are to have the same love, Paul said. That is, our hearts are all to be set on the same thing. Martin Niemöeller survived years in a Nazi prison camp with an even stronger faith. His visit to America drew great attention. Two newspaper reporters hurried to hear him, expecting a sensational discussion of those war years. Instead, Niemöeller shared a gospel message. The two reporters left the church disappointed. One said to the other, "Six years in a Nazi prison camp, and all he has to talk about is Jesus Christ."[1] Paul said we are to love Jesus so much that He is the theme of our lives and the heart of our conversation.

He said we are to be of one spirit.—Actually, the phrase "united in spirit" is the translation of one Greek word (*sunpsuchoi*). The word means "spirit with spirit." That is, our souls are to beat together in tune with Christ and with each other.

We are to think the same thing. We are to love the same thing. We are to want the same thing. We are to display a unity of mind, a unity of sentiment, a unity of spirit. We are to be one.

What is the distinctive mark of a Christian? How can we tell a person is a Christian? Is it by his assent to a particular creed? Some think so, yet many people who call themselves Christians have variances at one point or another in what they believe. Is it by his involvement in a certain worship ritual? This is the opinion of some. Yet, there are hardly two churches exactly alike in their approach to worship. Is the distinguishing point of a Christian life the moral tone of his actions? Morality is a part of

Christianity. Yet, some morally upright people do not claim the name of Jesus. What distinguishes a Christian from others? It is his inner desire to serve Jesus Christ.

That is the oneness about which Paul was talking. The way to get along, Paul said, is to get our mind and our heart and our spirit set on the one purpose for which we are here: to serve Jesus Christ and to glorify His name. When we all set our mind on that purpose, when there is unity on that matter, there will be harmony in the church. As William Barclay puts it, "No man can walk in disunity with his fellowmen and in unity with Christ."[2]

A Call to Humility (v. 3)

Paul's second directive is in verse 3. How do we get along with each other? Not only by harmony of mind, heart, and spirit, but also by humility. Paul presented this directive both negatively and positively.

Negatively, Paul said, "Do nothing from selfishness or empty conceit." This is similar to his declaration in Romans 12:3, that one should not "think more highly of himself than he ought to think." We should do nothing with the purpose of drawing attention to ourselves.

The word translated "selfishness" (*eritheian*) is an interesting word. It refers to a person who insists on *his* wages, *his* salary, *his* recognition. It refers to someone who is only concerned with his own vested interests.

The word translated "empty conceit" is the word *kenodoxian*. The word literally means "vain glory." It speaks of a person who seeks glory for himself but does not deserve that glory. An example is a young woman who went to confession at the Catholic church. She told the priest, "I want to confess my sin." The priest asked, "What is your sin?" She replied, "It is the sin of pride. Every morning when I look at myself in the mirror I realize how beautiful I am." The priest responded. "That's not pride. That's a mistake!"

Paul spoke of a person who was always looking out for his own vested interest, who thought he was more wonderful than he really was. Paul said "Don't be that kind of person."

The positive expression of this idea is in the next phrase, "with humility of mind, let each of you regard one another as more important than himself." Each of us is to climb down from the throne on which we sit and let someone else sit there. How that simple step would revolutionize our congregations! The only problems I have ever experienced in a church came when a person did not get credit for something he did or he did not have his way. If we would become more concerned about giving attention, credit, and praise to others than we are in receiving attention, credit, and praise for ourselves, if we developed the true spirit of humility, we would begin to experience a new quality of fellowship and unity.

President Ulysses S. Grant was on the way to a reception in his honor, in days before television allowed everyone near-instant recognition of the presidential face. He was caught in a rain shower and shared his umbrella with a stranger who was going to the reception, too. He said to Grant, "I have never seen Grant and I merely go to satisfy a personal curiosity. Between us, I have always thought that Grant was a very much overrated man." Grant replied, "That's my view also."[3] The same such view should characterize the life of every Christian. Thinking less of ourselves and more of Christ and others is the essence of humility.

A Call to Helpfulness (v.4)

We find the third directive in verse 4. How do we get along with each other? Paul said, "Do not merely look out for your own personal interests, but also for the interests of others." He issued a call to helpfulness.

I often tell a young couple during their wedding ceremony that to love someone means to say to them, "I want your problems to be my problems for as long as we live." Should not that also be the meaning of love between Christians? Because we have been brought together in the fellowship of love, we are to say to each other, "I want your problems to be my problems for as long as we live."

A well-known pastor some years back was going through a divorce. A newspaper reporter asked him about the response of the church to his divorce. He answered, "This church does not shoot its wounded soldiers." Do we? Do we shoot our wounded soldiers or do we compassionately nurse them back to health? Do we ignore the problems of others or are we sensitive to them? Do we add to each other's burdens or do we, as the Bible instructs, "Bear one another's burdens and, thus, fulfill the law of Christ"? (Gal. 6:2).

The secret to getting along is to always keep an eye out for the burdens of our brothers in Christ so we can lend a helping hand. We can demonstrate our helpfulness in three ways.

We need to recognize the need.—A man crawled away from a car accident, bloodied and bruised. Someone asked what he was doing. He responded, "I don't want to get involved." Such is often the pathetic picture of the church, crawling away from the dilemmas of life because we do not want to get involved. We *are* involved. We are part of the human dilemma, and we cannot escape it. Being a Christian means recognizing we have a responsibility to meet that need. The world has great need, and we Christians are responsible to deal with it.

We need to remove the conditions.—When a man entered a certain hotel he cut his finger on a sharp piece of metal protruding from the doorknob. He rushed over to the receptionist. "Can you help me?" he asked, "I cut my thumb on the door." She quickly supplied a napkin and bandage. He commented on her efficiency in dealing with his need. She replied, "Actually, I've had lots of practice. You are the third person today to cut his hand on that door." Three people had already been hurt on that door! Yet, no one made any attempt to correct the problem. They just doctored the cut fingers. How like the approach of the church to the problems of life. Part of our responsibility as Christians is to change the conditions which create human need.

We need to reclaim the life.—When the conditions cannot be removed and the hurt remains, we must reach out and minister to that hurt and thereby reclaim that life for God.

Fiorello La Guardia was one of New York's greatest mayors, partially because of his helpfulness toward people. One night he chose to preside over night court to see where people were hurting. Out of the cold night, a woman was brought before him for stealing a loaf of bread. She explained her family was starving. La Guardia said, "I have to punish you, for the law is the law. I fine you ten dollars." He then reached into his pocket and pulled out a ten-dollar bill and tossed it into his hat. "I'll pay the fine," he said, "and furthermore I'm going to fine everybody in this courtroom fifty cents for living in a town where a person has to steal bread in order to eat." He ordered the bailiff to collect the fines and give the money to the defendant.[4]

The secret to getting along is always to keep an eye out for the burdens of others so we can lend a helping hand. As we bear one another's burdens, our actions will provide the kind of fellowship that will enable us to stand together.

For Discussion

1. What things are threats to unity in the church today?

2. List some of the things God has done for you personally or for the church to which you belong. Share those with the group.

3. What are the personal spiritual goals for your life?

4. What does humility mean? How can we encourage humility today?

5. List the ministries to other people in which you are involved. What are some of your church's ministries to the needy?

7 | The Mind of Christ

Philippians 2:5-11

In 1896 Charles Sheldon, clergyman and author, wrote a book which eventually sold more than six million copies. His book has become a classic in the Christian literature of America: *In His Steps (or What Would Jesus Do?)*. In the story, the staid and comfortable worshipers of First Church were startled one day by the presence of a tramp. This vagrant had been in the city for three days, but had not received a kind word or help from any of a number of church members he had approached. He confronted the worshipers that morning with a disturbing question, "What do you mean when you sing, 'I'll follow Jesus all the way?' What do you mean when you say you are a follower of Jesus Christ? If you call yourself a Christian," the stranger said, "you should live like Christ." In response to the challenge of this stranger, the leaders of the church made a commitment to face every decision and confront every challenge with the question, "What would Jesus do, if He were in my place?" They made the commitment to follow in His steps. Charles Sheldon's book describes how that commitment changed their lives.[1]

Is it really possible for a Christian today to follow in Jesus' steps, to live as He lived and love as He loved and do as He did? Is it really possible to face every decision with the question, "What would Jesus do if He were in my place?" Paul explored that possibility in our text.

The Declaration (2:5)

Paul began in verse 5 with this bold declaration: "Have this attitude in yourselves which was also in Christ Jesus." The familiar *King James Version* is this: "Let this mind be in you, which was also in Christ Jesus." When Paul referred to the "mind" of Christ, he was not referring to Jesus' mental capacities. He was talking about His spirit, His demeanor,

His attitude. He was not saying, "Be as smart as Jesus." Rather, he was saying, "Act like Jesus. Approach life with the same spirit and the same attitude with which Jesus approached life."

The uniqueness of Jesus was not just in His mental capacity, His spiritual power, or His physical appearance. The uniqueness of Jesus was in the attitude with which He approached life. We can explain every accomplishment of Jesus' life, we can summarize every experience of His life with this simple statement: Jesus never quit loving people and He never quit trusting the Father. That attitude determined His achievement.

Paul challenged the Philippians to approach life with the same attitude Jesus had because he knew their attitude toward life would determine their achievement. This truth is repeated in other places in the Bible. For example, the Bible says, "For as he thinks within himself, so he is" (Prov. 23:7). A modern-day writer has said, "Your attitude toward your potential is either the key to or the lock on the door of personal fulfillment."[2]

Our attitude is the mind's paintbrush. It will determine how we see things, and it will determine the level of our achievement in life. Whenever we approach life with the attitude of the world, our usefulness will be nullified. Whenever we approach life with the attitude of Christ, our usefulness will be multiplied. Our attitude is the key.

Wally Westlake was a journeyman ballplayer, a .270 hitter who played ten years in the majors. During his travels around both leagues, he spent a little time with the St. Louis Cardinals. In the dugout one day Westlake went over to Stan Musial and said, "Stan, I gotta tell ya. I had a great night's sleep last night—I mean, a perfect night. I woke up this morning and my shower was perfect, the bacon and eggs were perfect. It was a beautiful day and my drive in to the ball park was just wonderful. I hit four home runs in batting practice. I'm in the lineup and I can't wait to walk up to the plate. I feel it in my bones. I'm gonna get three hits today. Did you ever feel that way?" Musial said, "Yes, every day."[3]

Paul said, "Every day, have this attitude in you which was in Christ Jesus," because the attitude with which we approach life will determine the level of our achievement in life.

How can we develop this attitude?

Remember Who We Are

According to the Bible, we Christians are not ordinary people. We are not cringing, fearful slaves. We are sons and daughters of God. Paul said to the Romans, "And so we should not be like cringing, fearful slaves, but we should behave like God's very own children. . . . For his Holy Spirit speaks to us deep in our hearts, and tells us that we really are God's children" (Rom. 8:15-16, TLB).

Remember Whose We Are

We Christians have been adopted by the omnipotent God who created and rules the universe. As a child of God, His power is available to us. The power which created the world and moves it toward its final destination, the power which through the centuries has brought life out of death and light out of darkness is available to us. The Bible says, "And since we are his children, we will share his treasures" (v. 8:17, TLB).

Because of who we are and because of whose we are, we Christians can face life with the same attitude Jesus had.

The Demonstration (2:6-8)

That raises an interesting question. "What is this attitude of Christ with which we are supposed to approach life?" Paul characterized the attitude of Christ with the word *humility*. The humility of Jesus was illustrated in two humiliations: the one by which Jesus became a man (vv. 6-7) and the one by which He became our Savior (v. 8).

The Incarnation (2:6-7)

Paul illustrated in these verses the humiliation by which Jesus became man. Notice, however, that Paul began with a declaration of the deity of Christ. He said, in verse 6, that Jesus "existed in the form of God." The word "form" (*morphe*) refers to the outward expression of the inner nature or character of something. The word "God" is without the definite article in the Greek text and therefore refers to the divine essence. Jesus' outward expression of His inmost being was an expression of the essence of God. Therefore, Paul said, Jesus was God. He possessed the very nature and essence of God in His own being. This passage, as others in the New Testament, declares the absolute and complete deity of Jesus Christ. Paul confirmed this in the next phrase in verse 6 where he declared that

Jesus possessed "equality with God." Jesus the Son was God just as God the Father was God. In every way and to every degree, Jesus shared the essence of deity.

Although Jesus existed in the form of God and possessed the essence of God, He did not consider that expression of deity as something He had to hold on to. Rather, Jesus "emptied Himself" (v. 7). Of what did Jesus empty Himself? Not His deity, for the word "existed" in verse 6 carries with it the idea of an antecedent condition projected into the present. Jesus was still divine after the incarnation. He still possessed deity. He did not empty Himself of the possession of deity but of the expression of deity. Instead of expressing Himself in the glory, power, and majesty of His deity, Jesus expressed Himself in the humility of a bondservant. By "being made in the likeness of men" Jesus exchanged the expression of His deity for the expression of humanity.

There is a mystery here our human minds cannot completely fathom. The basic truth is nevertheless inescapable. Jesus was God. He possessed deity, totally and completely. But He did not see that as something He had to hold on to, but rather He set it aside so He could express Himself in the form of a man in the incarnation. In so doing, Jesus illustrated the humility which was at the heart of His very being.

What does the incarnation mean?

The incarnation declares a truth *about Jesus.*

Two false ideas constantly challenge our understanding of Jesus. One false idea is the tendency to humanize Jesus to the degree that His divinity is lost. The other false idea is to divinize Jesus to the degree that His humanity is lost. The incarnation guards against both. The incarnation declares that we can never understand Jesus in any way which implies He is less than or inferior to God. Nor can we understand Him if we fail to realize that in all ways He was human as we are, except without sin. Jesus is/was fully God and fully human combined in one personality. That is the meaning of the incarnation. The Bible declares, "And the Word became flesh, and dwelt among us" (John 1:14).

The incarnation declares a truth *about God.*

In the incarnation God is revealed as a God who comes to us. An abyss between mankind and God has been caused by our sin. Our sin has separated us from God. However, God did not wait for us to approach Him, nor did He wait for us to take the initiative in the process of reconciliation. Instead, while we were yet sinners, indifferent and unconcerned, God took the initiative in coming to us. The incarnation declares that His love reaches all the way down to where we are.

The incarnation declares a truth *about mankind.*

A little boy, discovered in London after one of the bombings in World War II, was confronted with the reality of the loss of his family and the destruction of his home. His entire life had been uprooted. A minister was trying to find someone to whom the little boy belonged. In great despair, he said to the preacher, "You don't understand. I ain't nobody's nobody!" Many today face a crisis of insignificance. We have been dehumanized by the mechanistic nature of our computer age. Our lives have been disrupted by national and international affairs over which we have no control. We have been depressed by our age of the superstar when a person's worth is apparently measured by athletic prowess or physical beauty. The message of the incarnation is that we are all important to God regardless of who we are in the eyes of the world: we are no longer nobody's nobody. We are God's somebody.

The Crucifixion (2:8)

In verse 8 we see a second illustration of Jesus' humility. After He expressed Himself in the form of man, Jesus then humbled Himself further by voluntarily dying on the cross for the sins of man. Paul wrote, "And being found in appearance as a man, He humbled Himself by becoming obedient to the point of death, even death on a cross."

It was not enough for Jesus simply to take on human form. Mankind had a problem with which Jesus needed to deal: human sin. The result of this problem was separation from God. The need was for someone to pay the price for that sin and bring humanity back to God. God's plan for Jesus when He came to the earth was for Jesus to take upon Himself the sins of the world. When Jesus became a man, He was obedient to the plan. He willingly came to the earth as man. Then, He willingly died on the cross as man's Savior. From heaven to earth, from glory to shame, from master to servant, from life to death. What an amazing pathway Jesus followed![4]

Again this truth is shrouded in a mystery that cannot be completely comprehended by the human mind. The truth, however, remains. Although Jesus possessed all the privileges of manhood, He emptied Himself of those privileges and died on the cross as our Savior. In so doing, Jesus illustrated the humility which was at the heart of His very being.

How can we understand the cross?

We can understand the cross as a substitution.—The testimony of every person is that we are sinners. Consequently we deserve to die. But the good news which trumpets forth from Calvary is that Jesus Christ, the perfect Son of God, took our place. He died so that we might live. As Paul said to the Corinthians, "He made Him who knew no sin to be sin on our behalf, that we might become the righteousness of God in Him" (2 Cor. 5:21).

We can understand the cross as an illustration.—Sin is often whitewashed today, and preachers don't preach about sin as much as they used to. However, every time we begin to feel sin is harmless, we need to consider the cross and remember that our sin put Jesus there. The cross confronts us with the shattering reality of our sin. It reminds us that sin, when it runs its course, will destroy everything beautiful, good, and meaningful in life.

We can understand the cross as a revelation.—The cross has become the focal point of the good news, not because it illustrates the depth of our sin but because it also reveals the depth of God's love. Calvary was not just the result of man's perversion. It was also the result of God's plan. Jesus gave Himself freely, to die on the cross, according to the purpose of God, to make it perfectly clear how much God loves us. Paul said to the Romans, "But God demonstrates His own love toward us, in that while we were yet sinners, Christ died for us" (Rom. 5:8).

We can understand the cross as an invitation.—Why did the first Christian preachers focus on the cross? Why did Paul remind the Philippians about the cross? Because the cross is more than an illustration of the horror of sin and a revelation of the love of God, the cross has been an invitation to new life. Gipsy Smith (1860-1947), evangelist of the past, once said about the cross, "I am not afraid of the cross. I know that men used to come there to die, but since He died, they come there to live."[5]

The attitude with which Jesus approached life was an attitude of humility and hopefulness. He never stopped loving people and He never stopped believing in God. That attitude was illustrated in His willingness to become human and in His willingness to die on the cross as our Savior.

The Designation (2:9-11)

What happened to Jesus when He approached life with this attitude of humility? Paul answered that question in verses 9-11 in one of the most dramatic biblical statements of the Lordship of Christ. Paul said, "Therefore also God highly exalted Him, and bestowed on Him the name which is above every name, that at the name of Jesus every knee should bow, of those who are in heaven, and on earth, and under the earth, and that every tongue should confess that Jesus Christ is Lord, to the glory of God the Father."

When Jesus approached life with an attitude of humility, He emptied Himself of His expression of deity and became a man, and then He emptied Himself of His privileges as a man and died as our Savior. As a result, Paul declared, God exalted Jesus.

Mankind had done their worst to Jesus, but God honored Him. Mankind gave Jesus names of ridicule and slander, but God gave Him a glorious name. Mankind had buried Jesus, but God raised Him. When Jesus humbled Himself, God exalted Him and designated Him as Lord over all.

"Jesus is Lord" was the earliest confession of faith in the church. What does the lordship of Christ mean?

He Is Our Owner

To call Jesus Lord means He is our owner. To call Jesus Lord is to acknowledge that we belong to Him. He bought us and now He owns us. All our money, all our time, all our talents, all our relationships—everything belongs to Him. Paul put it like this in Romans: "For not one of us lives for himself, and not one dies for himself; for if we live, we live for the Lord, of if we die, we die for the Lord: therefore, whether we live or die, we are the Lord's" (Rom. 14:7-8).

He Is Our Master

To call Jesus Lord means He is our Master. As His servants, our only responsibility is to obey. To declare Jesus as Lord is to resign as the general manager of our lives and let Him take over. Abraham demonstrated this kind of obedience according to the writer of Hebrews who said, "By faith Abraham, when he was called, obeyed by going out to a place which he was to receive for an inheritance; and he went out, not knowing where he was going" (Heb. 11:8).

He Is Our God

Jesus is not only to obeyed as Master; He is also to be worshiped as God. That conclusion dawned on Thomas when, in the presence of the resurrected Lord, he fell to his knees and cried out, "My Lord and My God!" (John 20:28).

Conclusion

Every Christian is to approach life with the same attitude with which Jesus did. We are not to consider the privileges of our life as something to grasp, but we are to set them aside for the service of others. We are not to make the enriching of our own lives the ultimate aim of our living, but rather we are to be willing to give of our lives to others.

When we approach life with this attitude, when we have the "mind" of Christ, when we approach life with a spirit of humility, then God will exalt us, for the Bible says, "Humble yourselves, therefore, under the mighty hand of God, that He may exalt you at the proper time time" (1 Pet. 5:6). As a result, God is going to be glorified.

For Discussion

1. How can we develop the attitude of Christ?
2. What does the incarnation teach us?
3. How can we understand the cross today?
4. What does it mean to declare Jesus Lord of one's life?
5. What are some modern-day analogies to the concept of Lordship?

8 | Working Out Your Salvation

Philippians 2:12-18

According to the Bible, salvation is a gift given to those who have faith in Jesus Christ. I want to nail this truth down before we move forward in this chapter. If I don't, we might be confused by what Paul said in verse 12. When Paul said we must "work out [our salvation]," he did not mean that we must "work for" our salvation. How do we know that?

For one thing, these were Christians to whom Paul was writing. He called them "saints" (1:1), "beloved" (2:12), "citizens of heaven" (3:20, Phillips), and "brethren" (4:1). These were people who had already been saved. They could not work for their salvation because they already had it.

In addition, from beginning to end, Paul understood salvation, not as a work of mankind for God, but as a work of God for mankind. We find this truth all through his epistles. The most precise proclamation of this is in Ephesians 2:8-9. "For by grace, you have been saved through faith; and that not of yourselves, it is the gift of God; not as a result of works, that no one should boast." Salvation is not a reward for the righteous, not the wages for our work, but a gift for the guilty because of the grace of God.

Salvation does not come because of what we do but because of what Jesus has done, not because of the efforts of our lives but because of the efficacy of His death. Salvation is a gift. We do not earn it. We simply receive it. We experience salvation not by purifying our heart, not by perfecting our life, not by performing certain duties, not by providing certain services, but by simply believing in Jesus Christ and receiving Him into our heart. Salvation is a gift given to those who believe in Christ. With that truth nailed down, we are ready to hear what Paul said to the Philippians.

Realize the Potential Abiding in Us (2:12)

When we moved to Dallas, my wife and I spent the evening with some of our college friends whom we had not seen in a while. We pulled the college yearbook from the shelf, and began to go through the book, mentioning the different people whose pictures we saw. We had a great time, remembering and laughing. The sad note, however, was the realization that many young men and women of great potential in college had never realized that potential. Even sadder is the fact of Christians with great potential who never develop it.

The Bible affirms that Jesus not only saved us from something. He also saved us for something. Paul challenged the Philippians to realize the potential God placed within them. How could they do that?

The Action (2:12)

What did Paul want the Philippians to do? We see his desire in verse 12. Paul wanted them to "work out" their salvation. The Greek word translated "work out" is *katergazesthe*. What does that mean?

The Roman historian, Strabo, who lived in the first century before Christ and wrote in Greek, gave an account of the once-famous silver mines of Spain. He referred to the "working out of the mines" and used the exact word Paul used in our text. What did Strabo mean when he told his contemporaries to "work out the mines?" They were to operate the mines in a manner that would garner the utmost value from them. They already had the mines in their possession. Now they were to derive the full benefit from them.

The same Greek word was used in Paul's day, referring to a farmer working out his field in order to reap the greatest harvest possible. The seeds had already been planted. The crop was already growing. Now it was time to go out and harvest the crop. The farmer worked it out so he could gather a maximum harvest.

The Greek word actually means "to carry out to the goal, to carry to its ultimate conclusion." When we become Christians, God plants tremendous potential in our lives, like a mine or a field, and He wants us to realize that potential to its fullest. Working out the full benefit of our salvation is a task to which we must be committed every day of our Christian life.

The most dangerous misconception concerning salvation prevalent in the church today is the belief that at some point along the way we can retire from God's work, rest on our laurels, and live in the afterglow of yesterday's victories. For the Christian, there is no yesterday. We all live in an eternal today. What counts for God is what we do today. What is essential is how we serve God today. What determines our spiritual maturity is how closely we walk with God today.

One night at our Wednesday fellowship meal we shared around the tables. One of the things we shared was our favorite experience with the Lord. One of the ladies in my share group said, "Monday night, God did something special in my life." That's fantastic. She didn't talk about what God did when she was six or what God did ten years ago. She said, "Monday night, God was at work in my life."

Oliver Cromwell, English leader of the seventeenth century, wrote this motto in the front of his Bible: "He who ceases to be better, ceases to be good." That ought to be branded into the heart of every Christian. Are you closer to the Lord today than yesterday? Have you experienced more of the riches of God's mercy this week than last? Is God doing something in your life today? These are the questions every Christian should be asking himself. If the answer is "No," then we need to hear again the challenge of the apostle Paul to come out of retirement, climb out of our easy chairs, and begin working out our own salvation.

Salvation is not merely a great possession which God has committed to us. It is also a great program to which we must commit ourselves. We are to work out our own salvation. As Fred Craddock puts it, "The church is to actualize in concrete ways, in energy-burning, time-consuming endeavors, the mind of Christ."[1]

The Attitude (2:12)

How can we do that? Look at the next phrase in verse 12. For us to work out our salvation, we must approach the task with a particular attitude. Paul said we are to work out our salvation "with fear and trembling."

This phrase is the heart of our text. Paul's emphasis was not on working out our salvation but on "fear and trembling." These Philippian Christians wanted to experience God's best for them. They wanted to realize their full potential. Paul told them how to do it. It is to be done, Paul declared, "with fear and trembling."

What does this phrase "fear and trembling" mean? It means the recognition of who God is and who we are, the realization of His sufficiency and our impotency and thus, our total dependence on Him. It means constant apprehension of the deceitfulness of the world and the constant attention to the declarations of the Word. It means alertness to the things of the Spirit. It means the awareness that if we are not fully tuned into the things of God and totally committed to His way, we might miss something that God wants to do in us and for us.

To work out our salvation "in fear and trembling" means to be tuned into God, to be on His channel so that we can listen to Him. There will be no spiritual maturity, no realization of our potential, no working out of our salvation without that attitude of fearful dependence upon and sensitivity to God.

Release the Power Given to Us (2:13)

It will take more than just an attitude of fearful dependence and sensitivity to God to be able to realize our potential. Paul explained in verse 13: "For it is God who is at work in you both to will and to work for His good pleasure." Not only at the beginning, but at every point along the way in our Christian life, we are dependent on God's power.

In 1:28 Paul challenged the Christians in the church at Philippi to stand firm in the faith against outside threats. In 2:1-2 Paul urged them to get along with each other. In verse 5 Paul admonished them to have the same mind that was in Christ Jesus. In verse: 13 Paul called on them to work out their salvation. How can these things happen? Paul revealed the secret in our text. God's power makes it happen. God's power working in us enables us to stand firm. God's power working in us enables us to get along with one another. God's power working in us enables us to emulate the mind of Christ. God's power working in us enables us to work out our salvation to its fullest. That power is released in our lives by some simple steps.

Profession

We must publicly profess Jesus is our Lord and we belong to Him, for His power is available only to His children. Did you hear about the baby in New York which was fed elephant's milk, and the baby grew one hundred pounds in only a few weeks! Of course, it was a baby elephant to begin with. Only baby elephants can grow like that! Likewise, only Christians can experience the power of God working in and through their lives.

Involvement

We must participate actively in God's kingdom work to release the power of God in our lives. When Jesus said, "Where two or three have gathered together in My name, there I am in their midst" (Matt. 18:20), He was reminding us that God's power is somehow more effective when it is conveyed through Christians gathered together than in a Christian standing alone. Webster defines synergism as "the combined action . . . which is greater in total effect than the sum of their individual effects."[2] The principle of synergism also works in the spiritual realm. As we combine our efforts with the efforts of other Christians, the combined action is greater in total effect than the sum of our individual effects, because of the power of God.

Prayer

We must pray daily as we seek to sensitize ourselves to the things of the Spirit. Prayer puts us in a position where God's power can flow through us. All the way through the Book of Acts (1:14; 4:23-31; 12:5,12) prayer is the divinely ordained source of spiritual power.

When George Washington Carver appeared before a committee of the Congress, they asked him how he had made so many remarkable discoveries about horticulture. He explained, "I get up early in the mornings and I go out into the woods and listen for the voice of God."[3] Is it any wonder that this man experienced God's power in his life in a remarkable way? Time spent in the presence of God allows His power to flow more freely in and through our lives.

Study

We must study His Word to learn its truth and apply it to our lives. As we abide in His Word, God's power will abide in us. This was the truth Jesus shared with His disciples on the last night of His life: "If you abide in Me, and My words abide in you, ask whatever you wish, and it shall be done for you" (John 15:7).

Service

We must serve Him on a daily basis. God's power comes to those who are doing something for Him. When a person is confined to bed for a long period of time, the muscles will lose much of their strength. In contrast, when the muscles are stretched through extensive exercise, they will become stronger. That truth also applies in the spiritual realm. Spiritual inactivity will lead to the loss of spiritual strength. On the other hand, active service for the Lord will energize us spiritually.

As we publicly profess our faith in Christ, identify ourselves with God's people, pray daily to God, regularly study God's word, and serve God on a daily basis, then His power will flow through our lives and His power will enable us to realize the full benefits of our salvation.

Recall the Program Established for Us (2:14-16)

"Our character is revealed," says one modern quip, "by what we stand for, by what we fall for, and by what we lie for." How clearly the truth of this statement has been confirmed through the ages. The true character of many Christians has been revealed by the fact that they stand for nothing, fall for anything, and lie about everything. The need is for Christians with character, men and women who stand for something, men and women who will not lie about anything. The need is for Christians who live out in their lives the program Christ has established for us. How can we do this?

Keep Our Attitude Right (2:14)

Paul began verse 14 with a very simple, but much-needed, word for our day: "Do all things without grumbling or disputing." This command follows the command to obey in verse 12. Verse 12 has to do with the action; verse 14 with the attitude. Verse 12 tells the Philippians what to do; verse 14 tells them how to do it. They are to obey—without grumbling or disputing.

There is a kind of grudging obedience which presents the proper action without the proper attitude. For example, a little boy who was standing on the couch was told to sit down. He refused. His mother whacked him on the leg and said, "I told you to sit down." He still refused. Once more she whacked him, and this time he did sit down. But, with his arms crossed, he looked at his mother and said, "I'm sitting down on the outside, but on the inside I'm standing up!"

Many times that is the kind of obedience we give to God. We give our money to His work, but we say to ourselves, "I really don't want to give this money." We come to worship on Sunday morning, but all during the service we say to ourselves, "I wish I were at home watching the basketball game." That is the proper action without the proper attitude.

Paul encouraged the Philippians to obey with the right attitude, "without grumbling or disputing." The word "grumbling" (*goggusmon*) has to do with an unhappy spirit. Perhaps the allusion is to the conduct of Israel in the wilderness in Numbers 16:5,10, when they cried out against God and Moses. The word "disputing" (*dialogismon*) has to do with a questioning mind. An illustration of this was Satan's suggestion to Eve that God was lying to her and that she should not believe what God said (Gen. 3).

During World War II, the British General Montgomery was named commander of forces in North Africa for the purpose of rescuing Allied forces from a dreaded debacle. He met with his subordinates and told them, "Orders no longer form the basis for discussion, but for action."

That was Paul's sentiment. When we find out what God wants us to do through the revelation of His word or through the revelation of His Spirit in prayer, we are not to gripe about it. We are not to debate it. We are to do it! Do all things without grumbling or disputing.

Keep Our Life Pure (2:15)

The Philippians were to obey God with the right attitude so they could prove themselves to be "blameless and innocent." These two words describe two dimensions of integrity. Blameless (*amemptoi*) refers to what others think of us: our reputation. Innocent (*akeraioi*) refers to what we actually are: our character.

How can we have an inner character that is so unalloyed with evil that it will be manifest to those around us as being blameless? It will happen when we obey God, without complaint and without question. When we are obedient to God and develop this inner character that is outwardly displayed, Paul said we will be living like children of God.

Paul quoted from Deuteronomy 32:5 in this fifteenth verse when he spoke of a crooked and perverse generation. The children of God at that time were not acting like the children of God. Instead of obeying God, they were disobeying Him. Instead of doing what God told them to do, they were complaining. Instead of having an inner character that was outwardly manifest in blamelessness, they were crooked and perverse. God's children are not meant to be crooked and perverse, leading others astray. Instead, we are meant to be pure and undefiled. Children of God are not meant to increase the world's darkness. Instead, we are meant to be lights which illuminate the spiritual and moral darkness of our world.

A preacher asked a question I have never forgotten: "Are you a part of the problem or a part of the solution?" That was Paul's concern. We are children of God. We have been redeemed by the blood of the lamb and adopted into the family of God. We have the Spirit of God dwelling in us. We are not meant to be part of the problem, adding to the world's darkness. We are meant to be part of the solution, illuminating the world's darkness with the light of Christ which shines through us. Therefore, we need to keep our life pure.

Keep Our Witness Clear (2:16)

Paul told the Philippians to hold "forth the word of life"(KJV). We have the word of life, the gospel message, in our hands and we hold it out to the world, to present it to a lost and dying world so they can know the truth and come out of the darkness into the light. In verse 14 Paul urged the Philippians to obey God with the right spirit so they could witness to the world with their lives. Then, in verse 16, he told them to proclaim the word of God so they could witness to the world with their lips.

One of the most beautiful pictures of witnessing was given by a pastor of past generations named Halford Luccock. He was visiting the hospital in New Haven when a man came running down the corridor with a chart he had taken from the foot of a patient's bed. He grabbed Luccock by the arm and showed him the chart and said, "Look! Her temperature's gone!

Her temperature's gone!" Luccock said he did not know who the man meant by "her" but she must have been someone the man loved. He said he had never seen the man before and never saw him after that time. But, he said, to his dying day he would never forget the spectacle of a man so overwhelmed with good news that he had to grab the first stranger he saw and tell him about it.[4]

We Christians should be so overwhelmed with the good news of Jesus that we just have to grab the first stranger we see and tell them about it. We are to "hold forth the word of life."

Rejoice with the People Standing by Us (2:17-18)

One of the greatest benefits of the Christian life is that we do not stand alone. As we seek to realize our potential and release God's power within us and recall the program He established for us, we have around us others who are committed to the same goal. So Paul concluded this section by writing, "But even if I am being poured out as a drink offering upon the sacrifice and service of your faith, I rejoice and share my joy with you all. And you too, I urge you, rejoice in the same way and share your joy with me."

What is the source of our joy as Christians? Paul's joy did not come from the pleasant circumstances in his life. Paul was facing the possibility of death in the near future. He said, "That doesn't matter. I can rejoice, even if I die tomorrow." Paul did not find his joy in his own well-being.

Where did he find his joy? He found his joy in seeing the faithfulness of his Christian friends. He found his joy in their service for God, the growth of their faith, and their witness for Christ. He wanted the Philippians to find joy in his service for God and the growth of his faith. They should rejoice in each other's successes.

We need to learn that lesson today. I ran across an intriguing phrase recently. An author said, "It's hard to say 'amen' at someone else's prayer meeting." We can say "amen" at our own prayer meetings. We can rejoice when good things happen to us. We can be happy when our circumstances are good. But to say "amen" at someone else's prayer meeting, to rejoice when good things happen to others, to be happy when others' circumstances are good and ours are not—that is a deeper level to which most of us have not yet gone in our Christian lives.

As never before we need Christian men and women who will work out their salvation, Christian men and women who will realize the potential God has planted in us, open themselves to God's power, live the Christian life, and then rejoice in each other's successes.

For Discussion

1. What does it mean to work out our salvation?

2. How does our attitude affect our actions? Which is more important: our attitude or our actions?

3. Discuss the five steps which will help us realize God's power within us. How can you improve in each of these areas?

4. Why is holiness important in the life of a Christian?

5. Who was the most important person in leading you to make your decision for Christ? What person has the most positive influence on your Christian life today?

9 | Friends of Paul

Philippians 2:19-30

A certain merchant has a copy of this poem on the wall of his restaurant:

> Count your garden by the flowers,
> Never by the leaves that fall.
> Count your day by golden hours,
> Don't remember clouds at all.
> Count your nights by stars, not shadows,
> Count your life with smiles, not tears,
> And with joy on every birthday,
> Count your age by friends, not years.[1]

In a day when experts say only one American in five has a real friend, what a remarkable phenomenon was the man we know as the apostle Paul. His life was blessed with friends too many to number. Counting his life by his friends gives a true measure of the richness of Paul's life. We are introduced to two of his friends in the Letter to the Philippians.

Timothy (2:19-24)

Timothy was perhaps Paul's closest friend. Paul referred to him as "my true child in the faith" (1 Tim. 1:2) and "my beloved and faithful child in the Lord" (1 Cor. 4:17). Timothy is mentioned in the opening salutation of six of Paul's epistles, and two others are addressed to him. Raised in a culturally-mixed home with a Jewish mother and a Greek father, Timothy became a Christian and was used as a vital part of the early development of the church. In this letter to the Philippians, we see three qualities of Timothy's life.

He Was Competent (v. 20)

Paul said of Timothy, "I have no one else of kindred spirit" (v. 20). On first reading, Paul seems to be saying, "No one else is so much like me."

Timothy probably did have many of the qualities of the apostle Paul. We tend to imitate our mentor in some ways. But that is not what Paul said. Paul's thought is captured in the Moffatt translation: "I have no one like him." No one was as eminently qualified to do this job Paul had in mind as was Timothy.

Think of the scope of Timothy's experience and knowledge. Already as a child, Timothy was an eager student of the Scriptures, a teachable and obedient son (2 Tim. 3:15). As he grew up, Timothy was highly recommended by those who knew him best (Acts 16:1-2). Upon his conversion to the Christian faith, Timothy became a special deputy and fellow worker of the apostle Paul (Rom. 16:21). Timothy was set aside by God as a minister of the gospel (1 Thess. 3:2). Timothy was present when the Philippian church was founded (Acts 16:11-40), so he knew the Philippians well. In addition he subsequently visited the church on more than one occasion (Acts 19:21-22; 20:3-6; 2 Cor. 1:1).

Timothy was Paul's special friend, but Paul did not select him for this special assignment in Philippi because of the friendship. Paul selected Timothy because he was a natural for this job. He was preeminently qualified.

He Was Concerned (v. 20)

We see a second quality which led to Timothy's selection in verse 20. Timothy was not only competent. He was also concerned. Paul told the Philippians, Timothy "will genuinely be concerned for your welfare."

Some leaders know what needs to be done, and are qualified to do the job, but they step all over people in the process. Christian leaders must be different. We must not only know what needs to be done. We must also do the job with compassion. An oft-used statement captures this truth: "People don't care how much you know until they know how much you care." Timothy cared deeply about the Philippian Christians, and that's why Paul selected him. Timothy had both the skill and the compassion to get the job done.

He Was Committed (vv. 21-22)

Apparently Paul could have chosen some others for the job. He did not select them because, "They all seek after their own interests, not those of Christ Jesus" (v. 21). Here, as in so many other places in the

New Testament, we see a concern not just with what we do but also with why we do it. Paul indicted the other Christians at Rome because of their motives.

They were concerned with themselves instead of with others.—Two children were fighting over the tricycle. Finally, one of them said to the other, "If one of us would get off this tricycle, I'd have a lot more fun." That is the way many of us are in the church. Our primary concern is not for others. Our primary concern is for ourselves. We structure our entire life, we plan our entire agenda, so we can meet our needs and accomplish our goals. We are concerned with ourselves instead of with others.

They were concerned with the easy way instead of with Christ's way.— At a religious festival in Brazil a few years ago, a missionary was going from booth to booth examining the wares. He saw a sign above one booth: "Cheap crosses." That's the desire of many of us in the church. We want to be Christians, but we do not want it to cost us anything. We want to be leaders, but we are not willing to pay the price. We are concerned with the easy way instead of Christ's way.

In contrasting Timothy with these other possible leaders, Paul said about Timothy, "But you know of his proven worth" (v. 22). Timothy was no novice. He was still young, perhaps in his thirties, but he had already demonstrated his worth in the crucible of experience. The Philippians did not have to wonder about Timothy. He had a track record anyone could investigate. What did this track record show? It showed that Timothy served with Paul like a child serving his father.

Do you remember when your dad asked you to help him do something at a time when you really wanted to please him? How did you act? You did the work enthusiastically, willingly, and you did your very best because you wanted your dad to be pleased. That was the way Timothy served—enthusiastically, willingly, with his best effort. Why? Because he thought of Paul as his father, and he wanted Paul to be pleased with what he did.

Epaphroditus (2:25-30)

If you were making a list of the greatest men and women of the Bible, Epaphroditus would probably not be on the list. He was not a mighty leader like Moses, not a great king like David, not a distinguished prophet like Elijah, not a dynamic preacher like Peter, not a visionary leader like Paul. Yet, he was a friend of Paul's, and Paul gave words of commendation to this first-century Christian layperson. What kind of Christian was Epaphroditus?

A Stable Christian (v. 25)

What do we know about Epaphroditus? Paul described him with three terms in verse 25. He said that Epaphroditus was his "brother," his "fellow worker," and his "fellow soldier." Epaphroditus was one with Paul in sympathy, in work, and in danger.

Paul called Epaphroditus "my brother."—Our relationships with others are on one of three levels. Level one is the acceptance level. To accept others means to receive them graciously, to relate to them with kindness even if we are not in harmony with them and do not approve of everything they do. Level two is the agreement level. To agree with others means to be in harmony with them. We not only accept them in kindness, but we share some common aims with them. Level three is the approval level. To approve of others means to deem them satisfactory, to be in complete agreement with them. We not only accept them in kindness and share some common aims with them, but we are in complete sync with them. Our minds and our hearts are together with them.

Paul's reference to Epaphroditus as his brother put their relationship on the approval level. Paul said of Epaphroditus, "Our minds and our hearts are together. He wants what I want. He believes what I believe. We are united in faith. I approve of him (author)."

Paul called Epaphroditus "my fellow worker."—Many Christians believe the right things but never do anything to propagate what they believe. Not so with Epaphroditus. He was not willing merely to believe the right things. He wanted others to know what he believed. He was willing to move into action for the purpose of furthering the gospel of Christ.

The real test of our faith is to translate our theology into biography. Epaphroditus did that. He not only shared the faith with Paul. He also shared with Paul in the work necessary to propagate that faith. He was Paul's fellow worker.

Paul called Epaphroditus "my fellow soldier."—The soldier imagery used to be more popular among Christians than it is now. In the past, we sang with real gusto, "Onward Christian soldiers, marching as to war." Even though we don't sing that song much anymore, the imagery is still valid. It is found throughout the writings of Paul. We are at war with the forces of evil. Like dedicated soldiers, we must be willing to defend our faith.

Paul was constantly laying his life on the line to defend the faith. He said about Epaphroditus, "He shares with me in this as well. Like me, he is a faithful, dedicated soldier who defends the faith against all who would try to tear it down."

These three phrases—brother, fellow worker, and fellow soldier—picture a stable Christian. Epaphroditus enjoyed the fellowship with other Christians (brothers). Yet, he didn't spend all his time in fellowship. He was also committed to spreading the faith to others (fellow workers). Yet, he didn't spend all his time simply spreading the faith. He also recognized there were forces which were attempting to tear away the foundation of the faith. So he spent time defending the faith against these evil forces (fellow soldiers). Epaphroditus kept all three of these elements in balance. That gave stability to his life.[2]

Problems often arise today when we lose the balance, when we emphasize one or the other of these three elements.

Some people enjoy the fellowship so much they never do anything to share the faith with others. They are brothers but not fellow workers or fellow soldiers. As a result, they become self-centered and exclusive in their faith.

Others are so involved in sharing their faith and doing things for God they neglect the fellowship with other Christians. They are fellow workers but not brothers or fellow soldiers. As a result, they become individualistic and eccentric in their faith.

Others spend all their time defending the faith against every enemy, real and supposed. They never have a positive word to say. They are always striking out at somebody. They don't enjoy the fellowship of the church because they are afraid they will share fellowship with someone who is not as pure in their faith as they are. They are fellow soldiers, but not brothers or fellow workers. As a result, they become angry and belligerent in their faith.

How we need today in our churches more Christians like Epaphroditus, Christians who will keep the sharing, the working, and the defending all in balance, so they can be stable in their Christian lives.

A Serving Christian (v. 25)

Paul gave a second characteristic of Epaphroditus. Paul called him "your messenger and minister to my need." The word "messenger" is the word often translated *apostle*. This is someone who is sent out with an assignment. Epaphroditus was an official representative of the church at Philippi. What was his assignment? Apparently, he brought to Paul a gift to express the concern of the Philippians. While there he cared for Paul's needs. That is why Paul went on to describe him as minister to his need. Epaphroditus was sent to bring a gift to Paul and to be a gift to Paul.

The word translated "minister" is a Greek word from which we derive *liturgy*. A liturgy, according to the dictionary, is "a prescribed form for a public religious service."[3] This is an interesting idea. As Epaphroditus carried out his ministry to Paul, he was actually performing an act of worship to God. In other words, we worship not only by what we do in church on Sunday. We also worship by what we do for one another all through the week.

The implication of the text is that Epaphroditus carried out his assignment with the right spirit and in the right manner. He was not only a stable Christian. He was also a serving Christian.

A Sensitive Christian (vv. 26-28)

Paul was gracious for all that Epaphroditus had done. But now, Paul felt compelled to send Epaphroditus back to Philippi. Paul mentioned three reasons why he was sending Epaphroditus back to them.

He sent Epaphroditus back "for the Philippians's sake."—In verse 28 Paul told the Philippians, "Therefore I have sent him all the more eagerly in order that when you see him again you may rejoice." The Philippians were worried about Epaphroditus so Paul sent him back to relieve their anxiety.

He sent Epaphroditus back "for Paul's sake."—Also in verse 28 Paul mentioned a second reason for sending Epaphroditus back. Paul wrote, "Therefore I have sent him all the more eagerly in order that . . . I may be less concerned about you." As long as the Philippians were anxious and concerned, Paul was anxious and concerned. Because of his love for them, he felt what they felt. He hurt with them. So Paul said, "When

Epaphroditus gets back to Philippi and you realize he is all right and your fears are relieved, then I will feel better too."

He sent Epaphroditus back "for Epaphroditus's sake."—The main reason Paul sent Epaphroditus back is found in verses 26-27. Paul was sending Epaphroditus back because it was best for Epaphroditus. Paul wrote about Epaphroditus in verse 26, "He was longing for you all and was distressed because you had heard that he was sick."

When Epaphroditus reached Rome, he picked up some kind of sickness. We don't know what it was any more than we know what Paul's thorn in the flesh was. We can only speculate. Perhaps it was something Epaphroditus picked up because of his diligence in serving Paul. Maybe he stayed up day and night taking care of Paul, and then spent time sharing his faith with others, and perhaps had some debates with others about faith. Finally, in pure exhaustion, with his resistance down, he became ill. Whatever the sickness was, it was serious. We see this clearly in verse 27. Paul said, "For indeed he was sick to the point of death." The church in Philippi found out about it and became overly worried about him.

Epaphroditus, in turn, was worried because they were worrying about him. The word translated "distressed "(v. 26) is the same word used of Jesus at Gethsemane (Matt. 26:37). He was in deep distress because of the concern he was causing the Christians at Philippi. The only way the problem could be solved would be for Epaphroditus to go back home and show them he was well. Only then could the anxiety of Epaphroditus be allayed.

We see in this discussion that Epaphroditus was highly concerned about the Christians in Philippi. He was concerned about how they felt. He was concerned about their burdens. He was a sensitive Christian.

We have become so sophisticated and so controlled in our churches that we have to a large degree lost our sensitivity. I can remember as a preteenager crying whenever a person made a public profession of faith in Jesus Christ. My heart was touched. I haven't cried like that in a long time. How long has it been since you cried over someone else's need? How long has it been since you were emotionally moved by the concern and anxiety of others?

We see this sensitivity in some of the great saints of the past. Jonathan Edwards (1703-1758), the most effective preacher during the Great

Awakening, a mighty spiritual movement in early American history, often wept when he delivered his sermons. George Whitefield (1714-1770), the gifted colonial preacher, seldom preached without tears. One of the most powerful preachers in Scottish history was Robert Murray McCheyne (1813-1843). When someone asked the sexton the secret of McCheyne's success, he said that McCheyne let the tears flow. William Booth (1829-1912), the founder of the Salvation Army, preached a message after which hundreds responded to the gospel. After the service, an assistant found him in tears. "Why are you crying?" he asked. "Think of all the ones who came to Christ." Booth said, "I was just thinking of all the hundreds who did not come."

Epaphroditus fits into that tradition of Christians whose hearts were touched by the needs and concerns of others. He was a sensitive Christian.

A Sacrificing Christian (vv. 29-30)

In these final two verses, we see yet another quality of Epaphroditus. Paul said, "Therefore receive him in the Lord with all joy, and hold men like him in high regard" (v. 29). Paul said, "Epaphroditus is a special kind of person, a man who needs to be held in high regard." Why? Paul explained: "Because he came close to death for the work of Christ, risking his life to complete what was deficient in your service to me" (v. 30).

The key word is "risking" (*parabouleusamenos*). The word means to lay your life on the line, to stick your neck out, to tread where others fear to tread. It means to be willing to sacrifice.

This example of Epaphroditus was copied by others. In the early church some societies of men and women called themselves the *parabolani*. They were the riskers or gamblers. They ministered to the sick and imprisoned, especially those who were ill with dangerous and infectious diseases. They saw to it that, if at all possible, martyrs and sometimes even their enemies would receive honorable burial. They were willing to sacrifice themselves to give a cup of cold water in Jesus' name.[4]

How long has it been since we risked something for Jesus Christ? Or do we always play it safe? Epaphroditus was an adventurous kind of Christian. He was not a follower; he was a pioneer. He didn't follow a trail; he left a trail. He was willing to sacrifice for Jesus Christ.

When I read the story of this stable, serving, sensitive, sacrificing

Christian layperson of the first century, my heart cries out to God, "Lord God, give us a church full of people today just like Epaphroditus."

For Discussion

1. What does it mean to be a friend? Who is that kind of friend to you?

2. What made Timothy a good choice as Paul's special messenger?

3. How can we maintain a balance between fellowship, service, and defense of the faith?

4. How can we increase our sensitivity toward other Christians?

5. What have you sacrificed for the cause of Christ?

10 | A Profile of Paul

Philippians 3:1-14

Our day is characterized by an intense interest in celebrities. Magazines which give inside information on such people do well at the newsstand. Television shows which delve into the character, background, or family life of the famous proliferate. We seem to have an insatiable appetite to know what makes popular people tick.

As Christians, we often have that same interest in the heroes of our faith. None has provoked such intense interest over the centuries as the apostle Paul. What made him tick? What were the dynamics that made possible his productive life for Christ? Paul provided some unique insight into his personality in his personal letter to the Philippians.

Paul's Problem (vv. 1-3)

Strong personalities often arouse opposition as well as support. Such was the case with Paul. He was sharing the good news of God's love for a sinful world. Nevertheless, Paul had enemies. Although Paul was faithful to God and consistent in his commitment, he was constantly surrounded by enemies who tried to destroy him. These enemies were apparently Jewish leaders who were trying to convince Christians they had to follow the Old Testament law in order to become a Christian. Paul described these enemies with three words.

Dogs (v. 2)

Dogs may be mankind's best friend today. However, in the ancient world, dogs were more likely to be scavengers which roamed the streets, lived in the garbage dumps, and attacked everyone they met. The Jews of Paul's day called the Gentiles "dogs." Paul turned the tables on them, saying, "You are the ones who are dogs. You have defamed the name of God and have distorted the law of God."

What did Paul mean when he used this term to refer to his enemies? He was referring to the irrationality of their attacks and the unfairness of their accusations. Like scavenger dogs, they followed Paul and harassed him everywhere he went.

Evil Workers (v. 2)

The Jews believed righteousness was something which could be obtained from the outside in. Good works on the outside would make them righteous on the inside. Paul knew better. Righteousness could only be obtained from the inside out. An inside change, wrought by the grace of God, would manifest itself in outward righteousness. When the Jews proclaimed this false understanding, they were not leading people to righteousness but away from righteousness. Thus, Paul called them workers of evil.

False Circumcision (v. 2)

Circumcision was a sign among the Jews that they were a part of the people of God. They thought the symbol itself was enough to ensure their inclusion in the people of God, regardless of what was in their hearts. They overlooked their own Scripture which reminded them that circumcision of the flesh had value only when it was matched by circumcision of the heart (Lev. 26:41; Deut. 10:16; Ex. 6:12). Paul told his enemies, "If all you have is the circumcision of your flesh and it is not matched by circumcision of your heart, then you are not circumcised at all. You are mutilated."[1] The same idea appears in Romans 2:25 and Ephesians 2:11.

Whenever opposition arises against us or whenever we are confronted with undeserved and unexpected criticism, we are in good company! Paul had that problem, too.

Paul's Perception (vv. 4-7)

This outward criticism caused Paul to take a close look at his own life and determine his priorities. In this passage, Paul played the role of the accountant, balancing assets and liabilities, coming out with a bottom-line figure for his life. Let's look over his shoulder as he took his spiritual inventory.

From the perspective of the world, Paul had some things about which he could boast (v. 4). These were elements which needed to be entered on the balance sheet. He began to list those in verse 5.

His Pedigree (v. 5)

Paul focused first on his pedigree. Paul said, "[I was] circumcised the eighth day." Circumcision marked a man as being a part of the people of God. Converts to Judaism were circumcised in adulthood. Descendants of Ishmael were circumcised in their thirteenth year. Only pure-blooded Jews were circumcised on the eighth day. That's what Paul was.

Not only was he a pure-blooded Jew, but he also came from the right family. He was "of the nation of Israel, of the tribe of Benjamin." Paul's roots could be traced back to the tribe of Benjamin which was the tribe from which the first king of Israel came (1 Sam. 9:1-2). It was one of the two tribes which remained faithful to David when the kingdom of Israel split (1 Kings 12:21). It was also one of the tribes which formed the nucleus of the new Israel restored after the Babylonian captivity (Ezra 4:1). Paul was definitely from the right family.

In addition, Paul was "a Hebrew of the Hebrews." His family retained its Hebrew culture and continued to speak the Hebrew language instead of acquiescing to the pressures of the Greek cultures (Hellenism) which was so prominent in the world at that time.

What a family tree Paul had! He had the right bloodlines. He was a product of the right family. He had available all the advantages that accompany such a position of importance. That was the first element to enter on the balance sheet of his life.

His Credentials (v. 5)

"As to the Law, [Paul was] a Pharisee." We usually associate negative thoughts with the word, "Pharisee," but that was far from the case in Paul's day. Pharisees went to the right schools. They graduated from Palestine Prep School, the University of Jerusalem, and Moses' School of Theology.

Several years ago students from the University of Texas had orange decals on their cars which simply said, "The University," as if there were no other. That was the esteem associated with the Pharisees of Paul's day. He had the credentials.

His Achievements (v. 6)

Added to his pedigree and his credentials, Paul listed his achievements. This is the impact of the phrase, "as to zeal, a persecutor of the church." In every group of people, some are outstanding and others seem to be average in their achievement. So it was in the Pharisees. Some were at the top level and others existed on a lower level. The top Pharisees were those who not only followed the law of God, but also relentlessly eliminated anything which challenged their understanding of the law of God. Paul says, "That was me." He was a high achiever, a success, one who militantly opposed any threat to the Hebrew faith.

His Character (v. 6)

In addition, Paul also had character. Paul said, "As to the righteousness which is in the Law," he was "found blameless." The public life of some leaders is not matched by their personal life. Successful in the public eye, their personal life cannot stand up to the light of close inspection. Not so with Paul. The actions of his life were so closely aligned with the expectations of the law that he could be called "blameless." He was flawless in his character.

When Paul evaluated his life from the perspective of the world, he focused on his pedigree, his credentials, his achievements, and his character. The world considered these elements in Paul's life assets. Paul's enemies (3:1-3) evidently considered those elements life's greatest attainment. How did Paul evaluate them? The pivotal verse in the passage is verse 7. Paul said, "But whatever things were gain to me, those things I have counted as loss for the sake of Christ." The key word in this verse is the word "counted" (*hegemai*). The word, which appears three times in verses 7-8, means "to evaluate" or "to assess." Paul evaluated the things the world considered important—his pedigree, his credentials, his success, his character—and he decided these had no value at all.

Paul's Priority (3:8-11)

Because of his faith, Paul gave priority to certain things, and these were the qualities which he valued most highly.

Knowledge of Christ (v. 8)

The first element Paul called "the surpassing value of knowing Christ Jesus my Lord." That knowledge of Christ had to be entered on the balance sheet. The Greek word (*gnosis*) means knowledge gained through personal experience and intimate companionship.

We can know a person in four ways. We can know a person historically. We know Abraham Lincoln, George Washington, and Shakespeare in this way. All of our knowledge of them is drawn from history. We can know a person contemporaneously. We know George Bush, Queen Elizabeth, and Michael Jordan in this way. These people live contemporaneously with us. New facts are being uncovered about them every day. But all of our knowledge of them is drawn from a distance. We can know a person contactually. We know the teller at the bank and the clerk at the store and, usually, our neighbors in this way. We have contact with these people, our lives touch, and we talk with them, but our relationship never moves beyond a surface kind of experience. Or, we can know a person experientially. We know our husbands, wives, children, and special friends in this way. This is a deep kind of knowledge that comes out of personal experience and intimate communion. That is the kind of knowing Paul had in mind when he referred to the knowledge of Christ (v. 8). That personal, experiential knowledge of Christ was one of the factors Paul entered on the balance sheet of his life.

Righteousness in Christ (v. 9)

Another ingredient was the righteousness which comes from God on the basis of faith. All his life, Paul desired to be righteous and thus acceptable before God. Despite his attempt to keep the law, Paul did not feel accepted. Rather this thought often exploded from his conscience: "Wretched man that I am! Who will set me free from the body of this death" (Rom. 7:24). When Paul met Jesus on the Damascus road and received Him, Jesus gave him the very thing he desired. The clearest expression of how this process takes place is in 2 Corinthians 5:21: "He made Him who knew no sin to be sin on our behalf, that we might become the righteousness of God in Him."

Fellowship with Christ (v. 10)

Another factor to be considered in Paul's inventory was the fellowship with Christ. What did Paul mean when he mentioned "the fellowship of His sufferings"? Paul did not simply mean he experienced the physical suffering which Jesus endured, although 2 Corinthians 11:23-28 indicates he did. Paul did not simply mean he shared the spiritual anguish which caused him, like Jesus, to weep over the unbelief of his fellow Jews, although Romans 9:1-5 indicates he did. Rather, in the midst of those sufferings, Paul experienced the eternal, encouraging presence of the resurrected Christ. Paul knew that the depth of his suffering for Christ had been matched by the depth of his fellowship with Christ. Paul could not take an inventory of his life without considering that sweet, sustaining fellowship he experienced with Jesus Christ.

Promises from Christ (v. 11)

Paul also gave priority to the promises from Christ. Paul expressed the hope "that I may attain to the resurrection from the dead." Paul was not expressing doubt or uncertainty with the phrase "may attain." Rather, he was expressing humility. "May attain" conveys the idea of arriving at a goal. Paul was talking about the promise Jesus gave to Martha when He said, "I am the resurrection and the life; he who believes in Me shall live even if he dies, and everyone who lives and believes in Me shall never die" (John 11:25-26).

The things which the world considers important, Paul rejected as valueless. The things which the world rejected, Paul gave priority to. He said, "But whatever things were gain to me, those things I have counted as loss for the sake of Christ (v. 7)." "There was a time," Paul said, "when I put my pedigree, my credentials, my success, and my character on the asset side and the knowledge of Christ, righteousness in Christ, fellowship with Christ, and promises from Christ on the liability side. But then I put the pencil to it and the bottom line was zero." That's what the word "loss" means in verse 7. Paul was an auditor who opened the books of his life to see what wealth he had and discovered instead he was bankrupt.

Then a new factor appeared in Paul's life, Jesus Christ, and that completely changed the columns of loss and gain. The very things he thought were assets he moved to the liability side. The factors which he had thought were liabilities he moved over to the asset side. Then when he put the pencil to it again, he found that the bottom line was:

the PURPOSE of Philippians 3:14, "I press on toward the goal for the prize of the upward call of God in Christ Jesus":

the PRAISE of Philippians 4:4, "Rejoice in the Lord always; again I will say rejoice";

the PEACE of Philippians 4:11, "I have learned to be content in whatever circumstances I am";

the POWER of Philippians 4:13, "I can do all things through Christ which strengtheneth me" (KJV); and

the PROVISIONS of Philippians 4:19, "My God shall supply all your needs according to His riches in glory in Christ Jesus."

What a difference! From a negative bottom line to all those positive assets. From an empty life to a life full of the riches of God. From a life with no hope to a life with a future as bright as the promises of God. From being spiritually bankrupt to a spiritual millionaire. After Paul let Jesus Christ take charge of his life, rearrange his priorities, and restructure his ledger, the bottom line was never the same again. Paul found true wealth in Jesus Christ. Paul understood the immortal words of Jim Elliott, the missionary martyred by the Auca Indians: "He is no fool who gives up what he cannot keep, to gain what he cannot lose." Paul knew the things which deserve priority.

Paul's Persistence (3:12-14)

Because of the priorities to which Paul gave his life, he was able to persist through difficult times and overwhelming odds. Nowhere do we see his persistence so brilliantly expressed as in these key verses in the Philippian Letter. The greatest indictment of the Christians in our day is not that we are falling short of the mark but that we have quit striving to reach the mark. At no other point in the Bible do we see such an excellent example to emulate as we do in Paul.

His Awareness (v. 12)

Some, hearing the recitation of Paul's achievement in the preceding verses, might be tempted to say, "Well, Paul, you've done it all. You have it made. There is really nothing more you can do." Immediately Paul presented two qualifiers on his life. He said, "Not that I have already obtained it," and "not that I . . . have already become perfect."

What did Paul mean when he said, "not that I have already obtained it"? The scene is that of a race in the ancient world. Picture an ancient Greek stadium with its course for footraces and tiers of seats for the spectators. In the ancient stadium, the contestants lined up on stone blocks which contained grooves to give the sprinter's feet a firm hold for a quick start. Here the contestants waited, body bent forward, one hand lightly touching the ground, awaiting the signal. When the signal was given, the contestants raced toward the goal. After the race was over, the winner was given a wreath recognizing his achievement. The "it" Paul referred to was the wreath given at the end of the race. Paul was saying "I know that the race is not over yet. I have not yet done all that God has for me to do."

Look at the other qualifier. Paul said, "Not that I . . . have already become perfect." The word translated "perfect" is the Greek word, *teteleiomai*. It comes from a verb which means "to reach the end," or "to bring fulfillment." Paul was saying "I know I have not yet become all that God wants me to be. I have not yet fulfilled my potential." How we need to face each new day with this awareness: "I have not yet done all that God has for me to do. I have not yet become all that God wants me to be."

His Ambition (3:12)

Facing each day with that awareness led Paul to write, "I press on in order that I may lay hold of that for which also I was laid hold of by Christ Jesus." Some who realize they have not done all that God wants them to do and have not become all that God wants them to be respond with despair. They are ready to give up. Paul responded with determination. He was ready to press on.

Implied in Paul's statement is the fact that Jesus has a plan and purpose for each of our lives. When Jesus saved us, He saved us for a purpose. He laid hold of us for a reason. Paul recognized that truth. God had something special for his life, something he had not realized in all of its fullness. So Paul said, "I press on so I can claim all that Christ has for me."

His Actions (vv. 13-14)

In verse 12 we see the awareness with which Paul approached life and the ambition he had for life. In verse 13, we see the actions that grew out of that awareness and ambition. Paul said, "Brethren, I do not regard myself as having laid hold of it yet." Some scholars suggest that the Philippians were being hounded by some pious saints who claimed to have attained perfection. Paul said, "That's not my experience. They may claim to be perfect but I'm certainly not. I have not yet reached the goal God has set for my life, so these are the actions I commit myself to each new day."

Before we look at those actions to which Paul committed himself, notice the intensity of his commitment. He said, "This one thing I do"(KJV). *The Living Bible* translates it, "I am bringing all my energies to bear on this one thing." Paul concentrated all his energy and attention on the work Jesus Christ called him to do.

The problem with most of us is not that we do not love Jesus. We do. Our problem is not that we do not want to live for Him and do His work and get involved in His church. Most of us do. Our problem is that our time, energy, money, and interests are diverted in a hundred different directions. We are involved in a multitude of good things and somehow our commitment to Christ just becomes lost in the shuffle. Our primary problem is our failure to concentrate on Christ and His work.

Paul learned the secret of concentration. "This one thing I do," he said. On what did Paul concentrate? In verse 13 we see two different actions on which he concentrated his attention, one negative and the other positive.

Paul concentrated on releasing the past.—One of the biggest barriers to enjoying all Christ has for us today is our unwillingness to release those things that happened yesterday.

Some people cannot release from their minds the accomplishments of the past. Many people live on their past accomplishments, on a blessing of God in their early childhood, on a cherished memory of yesteryear when they were on a spiritual mountaintop, on a moment when they made a bold stand for Christ in the past. Paul had plenty of spiritual mountaintops in his past to which he could have retreated. But Paul said,

"I am forgetting those good things of the past so I can reach out for the better things that are ahead."

Some people cannot release from their minds the hurts of the past. Many spend all their time fondling and nursing some wound of the past, some secret hurt which has so focused their minds on the past that it consumes all their energy in the present. Paul had a few hurts of his own he could have remembered. His entire ministry was carried out under the open hostility of those around him. Paul experienced misunderstanding, slander, and constant harassment. Paul could have nursed those hurts and sulked in his hatred. But he didn't. Why? Because he learned how to release his hurts of the past.

Some people cannot release from their minds the failures of the past. At a hundred different points this last month, we made mistakes of one kind or another. All of us had blunders which marred our efforts. We all had those experiences of denial, when, like Simon Peter in the courtyard, we look up to see the hurt in Jesus' eyes and feel so guilty we want to die. Think of Paul's past. Think of the harm he had done to the kingdom of God. Think of his part in the death of Stephen. Yet Paul said, "I am forgetting those things that are behind, and I am reaching out for those things that are ahead."

The past of every person is marked by spiritual victories and spiritual defeats, by personal friendships and personal feuds, by healing relationships and hurtful ones. But the past is behind us. It is gone. It has been entered into the logbook of life and we can do nothing about it now. So Paul said, "I concentrate my attention on releasing those things in the past which will keep me from doing what God wants me to do and becoming what God wants me to be in the present."

Paul concentrated on reaching for the future.—The negative approach to life is not enough. Just releasing the experiences of the past is not enough. There must also be a positive thrust in our lives. So Paul said he also concentrated on reaching forward to what lies ahead. Paul believed there were always more mountains to climb, more lives to help, more churches to build, more personal victories to win, more sermons to preach, more work to be done. "I count not myself to have apprehended" (KJV). he said. He still had much of the race to run, so he kept running.

One of the problems in the church today is that we have too many Christians who have given up too soon. Too many of us have retired, hung up our spiritual uniforms, taken a sabbatical, and sat down under the shade of the old apple tree to wait for the Lord to come, when we ought to be out still running the race. We teach a class for a few years, and then, we are ready to quit. We've done our part. We witness to someone one time and are rejected, so we quit. We've done our part. We make a few phone calls, write a few letters, keep up the work for a while, and then we quit. We get excited about visiting, but no one else shows up, so we just quit. We want to be in the choir and practice for awhile, but then we get tired and just quit. Millions in the church today feel like they have done their part, run their race, and finished their course, when, in reality, they have not even made it through the first lap.

Like Paul we need to learn our lessons from the past and release the past. Then, we need to reach out for the future adventures and experiences God has waiting for us.

For Discussion

1. Do you have any enemies? How should we respond to our enemies?
2. Make a spiritual balance sheet on your life, listing on one side of a piece of paper your liabilities and on the other side your assets. Discuss with the group.
3. What is the top priority in your life? How do you demonstrate your commitment to that priority in your everyday life?
4. What are some areas in your Christian life that need to be developed?
5. What personal goals have you set for your life?

11 | Learning How to Walk

Philippians 3:15-21

A welfare worker was sitting at her desk, looking out the window at some children playing ball in a vacant lot. A badly crippled little boy sat watching the children play. The welfare worker went down to the ball field and talked to the little fellow. She discovered he had broken a bone when he was hit by a car, but he had not been taken to the hospital to have the broken bone straightened because his family did not have the money. The welfare worker took the boy to a famous physician who agreed to do the operation free. The bone was rebroken and properly set, and after some months the boy could walk and run as well as any of the other children. The welfare worker was proud that she was responsible for helping the lame boy to be healed. Years later she was telling this story to a women's club. She said, "Would you like to know where that boy is today? He is in the state penitentiary. I was so busy helping him to run that I forgot to teach him how to walk."

It is essential that we as Christians learn how to walk. Paul gave some helpful instructions in our text. According to Paul, the Christian walk is marked by three things.

A Holy Discontent (vv. 15-16)

Paul said, "Let us therefore, as many as are perfect, have this attitude" (v. 15). The word translated "perfect" is the Greek word *teleioi*. The word means full grown instead of being a baby; mature instead of imma-ture. The word means whole rather than incomplete. Paul said a person who is full grown, mature, and whole has this attitude. What attitude? The attitude he described in the preceding verses, the understanding that we have not yet become whole or mature.

Notice the marvelous play on words in verse 15. A sign of being mature is the recognition we are not yet mature. A person who is spiritually mature realizes he is not yet mature. Therefore, a mature Christian does not retire from the Christian walk. Instead, he presses on in his Christian life because he knows he has not reached his destination. He knows there are still many miles to travel before he reaches home.

Paul continued his challenge with this statement, "However, let us keep living by that same standard to which we have attained" (v. 16). To what standard was Paul referring? The standard of perfection which none of us have yet achieved. We must always be humble in our evaluation of ourselves and diligent in our desire to improve ourselves because we know we have not yet become all God wants us to be. The Christian walk is to be marked by a divine discontent.

A Word to the Impressed

This word from Paul speaks to those of us who have a higher opinion of ourselves than we ought to have. Sometimes, when we think we have arrived, we are reminded we are not yet there.

A lad came up to former President Herbert Hoover just after he had left the office and asked for his autograph. When Hoover graciously complied, the little fellow said, "Would you mind signing it again, further down?" "All right," the President said, "But why twice?" "Because," the bright young businessman replied, "with two of yours I can get one of Babe Ruth's."

No matter what we attain in life, we will never reach perfection, so we need always to be humble in our evaluation of ourselves.

A Word to the Depressed

This word from Paul instructs those of us who have a lower opinion of ourselves than we ought to have. The problem with many today is not an inflated ego but a deflated ego.

A little girl's mother found her crying because a poor family down the street had moved away. The mother said, "I didn't know you cared so much for those children." The little girl responded, "It's not that I like them so much. It's just that now there is nobody that I am better than."

No matter how insignificant we seem to be, we can always become better, so we need to be diligent in our desire to improve ourselves.

How should we walk as Christians? We should walk with a divine discontent, realizing we have not yet reached maturity, but are always moving toward it.

A Healthy Defense (vv. 17-19)

Because the Christians at Philippi were surrounded by immorality, they needed a concrete example of Christian devotion. They needed a model to follow. Paul said, "Join in following my example and observe those who walk according to the pattern you have in us" (v. 17). Paul wanted the Philippians to follow him because all around them were people who sought to lead them away from Christ. Paul said, "For many walk, of whom I often told you, and now tell you even weeping, that they are enemies of the cross of Christ" (v. 18).

Who were these enemies of the cross? Were they members of the church who were not really Christians? Or were they people outside the church who were clearly identified as nonbelievers? We cannot tell from the text. Commentators are divided on their opinion of this matter. Whether these people are inside the church or outside the church, two things are apparent.

The presence of these enemies of Paul in Philippi broke Paul's heart. As Mary of Bethany wept at her brother's death (John 11:31), as Mary Magdalene wept on the morning of Christ's resurrection (John 20:11), Paul wept at the danger confronting the Philippians. Paul not only had a magnificent mind and a rugged constitution. He also had a tender heart.

In addition, the presence of these enemies of Paul in Philippi endangered the work of Christ in that city. These people stood in opposition to everything Paul stood for. They had declared war on the cause of Christ. Therefore, Paul urged the Christians at Philippi to have a healthy defense against them.

Paul described these enemies of the cross in verse 19 with four phrases.

Their Future (v. 19)

Paul said about these who opposed the work of Christ: "[their] end is destruction." Destruction does not mean annihilation. Paul did not suggest these people would cease to exist. The destruction Paul had in mind was a spiritual destruction. By opposing Christ and His work, these people forfeited the opportunity to become what God made them to be. They lost the opportunity to be in fellowship with God and with His people. Therefore, they would be separated from God through all eternity.

The greatest tragedy of hell is not its pain or its temperature but its length. It is everlasting destruction. Spiritual death was the ultimate destination of the road on which these enemies of the cross were traveling.

Ernest Hemingway lived a life of total disregard for the laws of God. He drank heavily, lived with different women, and lived a life of wanton recklessness. In 1956 a magazine said of Hemingway, "People with different ideas about morality would call him a sinner, and the wages of sin, they say, is death. Hemingway has cheated death time and time again, to become a scarred and bearded legend, a great white hunter, a husband of four wives, a winner of Nobel and Pulitzer prizes. Sin has paid off for Hemingway." However, the end of Hemingway's life was marked by despair and disillusionment. He attempted suicide several times. He spent many weeks in Mayo Clinic where he babbled around at about 70 percent of his mental efficiency. He developed a deep sense of paranoia. Eventually, he took his own life.[1]

Those who oppose the work of God may cheat death for a while. Eventually, the road they are traveling will lead to destruction.

Their Futility (v. 19)

Two phrases describe the futility of these enemies of the cross. The reason for their futility is found in the first phrase: "[their] god is their appetite." The word "appetite" includes all of the desires of the human body, not just hunger. These enemies of the cross did not control their appetites but rather were controlled by their appetites.

The pernicious myth of freedom leads many unsuspecting people down the pathway which eventually robs them of their freedom. They believe separation from God will lead to freedom. They discover, too late, that separation from God costs them their freedom. When they turn from God's control in their lives, they come under the control of their passions, appetites, and desires. The result is a life of futility.

The result of their futility is found in the second phrase: "those whose glory is in their shame." Because they lost their freedom to live for God, they did not find glory in being pure, kind, or good. They found glory in being as coarse, vulgar, and gross as they could be. They did not feel guilty about their immorality. They gloried in it. The pathway away from

God not only leads to the loss of freedom. It also leads to the loss of dignity.

A pastor friend of mine told of a young man he encountered one weekday in the sanctuary of the church. The young man was kneeling at the altar. The pastor watched him and when he arose to leave, the pastor approached him to see if he could help. As they talked, the young man described a life of sexual permissiveness which had begun at the age of thirteen and which had totally dominated his life. The pastor shared with the young man about God's love and God's power. He encouraged the young man to come to worship on Sunday. The young man attended church a few times but finally disappeared. A few days later the pastor received a note from the young man which said, "I tried, but I just can't break loose." He had the desire to come to God, but his sin had so taken control of his life, he could not break loose.

Those who oppose the work of Christ may enjoy themselves for a while. Eventually, the road they are traveling will lead to despair.

Their Focus (3:19)

How do people become enemies of the cross? Paul said "[they] set their minds on earthly things." A famous philosopher once said, "We are what we eat." The Bible suggests we are what we think. What we set our mind on, what we think about, what we concentrate on will determine what we become. These enemies of the cross set their minds on earthly things.

The Watergate scandal happened many years ago, yet its shadow still falls across American life. One of the key figures was Jeb Stuart McGruder, a promising politician with a strong background and a bright future. Yet, he became a part of the coverup surrounding the Watergate incident and eventually was sentenced to prison. When asked why he did it, McGruder responded, "My ambition obscured my judgment. Somewhere between my ambition and my ideals I lost my compass."[2]

The ambition of those who oppose the work of Christ obscures their judgment and prevents them from correctly evaluating God. Instead of identifying with God, they choose to oppose Him.

Paul warned the Philippians to avoid following these enemies of the cross. Instead, Paul wanted them to follow his example and the example of "those who walk according to the pattern you have in us" (v. 17). To whom was Paul referring when he mentioned "those who walk according to the pattern you have in us"? He was referring to the Christians who were faithful to Christ, Christians who look up instead of down, who look forward instead of backward, who look outward instead of inward. Paul described these upward, forward, outward looking Christians in the final two verses of the chapter.

A Heavenly Direction (3:20-21)

Paul told the Philippians "our citizenship is in heaven." The word for "citizenship" is the word from which we receive our English word *politics* and *political*. It has to do with our allegiance and identification.

To the Philippians this was a powerful image, for Philippi was a Roman colony. They considered themselves to be citizens of Rome although they lived in Philippi. They were a fragment of Rome. Therefore, they lived like Romans. They wore Roman clothing. Roman magistrates governed, and Roman justice was administered. They spoke the Latin tongue and observed Roman morals. Just as the Roman colonists never forgot they belonged to Rome, Paul urged the Philippians never to forget they belonged to God.

As Christians our focus, allegiance, and identification are with heaven and what it stands for. This does not mean to be so heavenly minded that we are no earthly good. To be heavenly minded does not mean to be dreamy, impractical, or distant. To be heavenly minded means to make a choice as to where we will give our attention and our allegiance.

Moses refused the pleasures and treasures of Egypt because he had something infinitely more wonderful to live for, God's cause (Heb. 11:24-26). This is what Paul was talking about. Every person has to make a choice as to how he will walk, where he will walk, and for whom he will walk. We can set our minds on the things of the world or we can set our minds on the things of God. We can be enemies of the cross or citizens of heaven.

Why should we chose to be citizens of heaven rather than identifying with the things of this world? Paul gave two reasons in the closing part of our text.

His Eventual Victory (v. 20)

Paul said we should choose Christ over the world because at His second coming He will claim His victory over the world. "We eagerly wait for a Savior, the Lord Jesus Christ" (v. 20) because we know He will eventually "subject all things to Himself" (v. 21). Someday Christ is going to return. At that time the kingdoms of this world will come under the control of Christ and His kingdom and He will reign for ever and ever (Rev. 11:15).

Steve Brown tells of a church in Czechoslovakia which was harassed by the government. Finally, the government closed the church and building and the members were forced to find another church house. They tried everywhere, unsuccessfully. Finally they purchased an old, broken-down building in the middle of a cemetery. They called their church, "The Church of the Resurrection."[3]

That is the essence of the gospel, the promise of eventual victory in the midst of circumstances which seem to promise defeat, the hope of eventual life in the midst of circumstances which speak of death. Because Christ will eventually be victorious, we need to align our lives with Him.

His Eternal Value (v. 21)

Paul said we should choose Christ over the world because the things of the world are temporary, while the things of Christ are eternal. This returning Christ "will transform the body of our humble state into conformity with the body of His glory, by the exertion of the power that He has even to subject all things to Himself" (v. 21).

One of the saddest experiences for a pastor is to stand by the bedside of a person whose physical body is wasting away. However, our physical bodies are not for eternity. They are for now. In one way or another, at one time or another, the physical body of each of us will die and be placed in a grave. Christ offers a spiritual body which is not temporary but eternal.

F. B. Meyer (1847-1929), gifted English preacher of another generation, wrote to a friend a few days before he died. He wrote, "I have just heard, to my surprise, that I have only a few more days to live. It may be that, before this reaches you, I shall have entered the palace. Don't trouble to answer. We shall meet in the morning."[4]

Choose the world and a day is coming when you will have to give up everything you have. Choose Christ and you have something which will never be taken away, an eternal relationship with God which even death cannot destroy.

For Discussion

1. What are some areas in your life with which you are not satisfied?
2. How does pride get in the way in the operation of the church?
3. What can we do to protect ourselves from outsiders who tempt us to turn away from our faith?
4. What is the one factor which more than any other determines what we become?
5. What did Paul mean when he said our citizenship is in heaven?

12 | The Fellowship of the Church

Philippians 4:1-9

Charles Swindoll suggests the real need in our world today is shelter for storm victims. He believes the church should fill that need. Therefore, churches need to be less like national shrines and more like local bars. They need to be less like untouchable cathedrals and more like well-used hospitals. They need to be places where a person can take his mask off and let his hair down, places where a person can have his wounds dressed and his broken life put back together again. To illustrate his point, Swindoll told of a conversation with a Marine buddy of his who had recently become a Christian. Swindoll asked him what he thought about the church. This was his reply. He said, "the only thing I miss is that old fellowship all the guys in our outfit used to have down at the slop shoot . . . we'd sit around, laugh, tell stories, drink a few beers, and really let our hair down. It was great!" The new Christian continued, "But now I ain't got nobody to tell my troubles to, to admit my faults to. I can't find anybody in church who will put their arms around me and tell me I'm still okay." Then he closed with: "Man, it's kinda lonely in there!"

When Luke described the first-century church, he said they devoted themselves to fellowship (Acts 2:42). That is an essential ingredient of the church. The sad truth is that often this fellowship is missing from the contemporary church. Instead of being a support society, the church becomes a courtroom in which all of the not-quite-perfect people in the world are judged. For many today, instead of being a place of refuge, the church is a lonely place.

Paul gave some needed instructions in the closing chapter of his Philippian letter on how to develop the fellowship of the church.

Stand Firm (v. 1)

Paul's first challenge to the Philippians was to "stand firm in the Lord." The Greek word for "stand firm" (*stekete*) pictures a soldier standing fast in the heat of the battle, with the enemy surging down upon him. He does not run. He does not retreat. He does not buckle under the pressure. He does not give up. He stands firm. This verse is a challenge to every Christian to stand firm in his faith. We are to stand firm when criticism comes, and the easiest thing to do is to give in. We are to stand firm when failure comes, and the simplest solution is to give up. We are to stand firm when disaster strikes, and we are ready to give out. Paul said we are to stand firm.

How can we do that? Paul gave two answers.

Remember

The first answer is found in the opening word of verse 1: "Therefore." That is a connective word. It links up with what has just preceded. In Philippians 3:20 Paul talked about our provisions as citizens in God's kingdom. In verse 21 Paul talked about our promises as children in God's family. When we remember all God has done for us through His provisions and promises, we are able to stand firm.

At the age of seventeen, I began to sense God's call to the ministry. Up to that point in my life, my only ambition had been to become a medical doctor. This new desire did not hit me all at once in a "Damascus-road" experience. Instead, it was a growing awareness which built over a period of several months. I spent many hours with Clyde Herring, my pastor. Through our prayers and discussion together, God began to make His will clearer in my life. We set up a youth-led service in which I was to preach. Although my "twenty-minute sermon" ended up being less than ten minutes long, God blessed that service in an unusual way. The response of the people, both during the service and after, confirmed God's call for my life. Since that time, whenever uncertainty comes to my mind, I always remember that experience in which God made His will unmistakably clear. By remembering what God did then, I can stand firm now.

Relate (4:1)

The second answer is found in the closing phrase of the challenge: "in the Lord." That is a relational word. It links us with the Lord Jesus

Christ. As we walk with the Lord, as we continually exercise our faith in the Lord, then we will have the strength to stand firm.

Have you heard the story of the aggressive vacuum-cleaner salesman who decided to make some calls along a country road. He knocked on the door of one house and the lady of the house opened the door. Before she could say anything, he rushed into the house and emptied a bucket of dirt on her floor. He said, "Ma'am, this is the finest vacuum cleaner ever made. It is so powerful it almost sucks up the carpet. If this vacuum cleaner does not pick up every bit of that dirt, I will eat it with a spoon!" Without a word, the woman turned and left the room. The salesman said, "Lady, where are you going?" She replied, "To get a spoon. We ain't got no electricity in this house!"

We have no power in the Christian life apart from our connection with the Lord. As we stand in Him, we can stand firm.

Stand Together (vv. 2-3)

We see a second challenge in verses 2-3. Paul challenged Euodia and Syntyche and the other Philippian Christians to stand together.

What beautiful names these two women had. Euodia means "prosperous journey" and Syntyche means "good luck." These two women in the Philippian church were known as Prosperous and Fortunate. Evidently, at one time, these women labored together with Paul for the cause of Christ. The ministry of women is a prominent feature of early Christian work, particularly at Philippi. These two women along with the other Christians at Philippi assisted Paul in establishing the church in that city. But then something happened. We do not know what. Some commentators suggest these two women represented the two racial groups in the church, and the Gentile members rallied around one of these women, the Jewish members around the other. Whatever the issue, these two women who had worked side by side in cooperation were now standing face to face in confrontation.

What was Paul's challenge to these two women? He said, "I urge Euodia and I urge Syntyche to live in harmony in the Lord" (v. 2). The word translated "urge" is an interesting Greek word. It comes from *para* which means "alongside of" and *kaleo* which means "to call." Paul called each of these women to line up alongside him and each other. They were to "live in harmony." The Greek words translated "live in harmony" literally mean to be of the same mind. That is, Paul not only challenged the Philippians to stand firm, he also encouraged them to stand together.

Paul did not imply that the Philippians should become exactly alike or for them to carry out the same function in the church or to perform the same ministry in the church. Paul wanted them to put their minds on the same matters, to have the same purpose, to be motivated by the same passion. He wanted them to share an obsession to serve the Lord Christ and further His cause. When we keep our eyes off of each other, and focus our attention on Christ, we will be able to stand together.

Stand Joyfully (v. 4)

Paul gave a third challenge to the Philippians in verse 4. He said, "Rejoice in the Lord always; again I will say, rejoice!" The word "rejoice" suggests the way every Christian should face life. Some people face life with such pessimism. They find a cloud in every silver lining.

For example, when the first American steamboat, Robert Fulton's *Clermont*, was scheduled to make its trial run on the Hudson River, a crowd gathered to watch the spectacle. One of the spectators was a pessimistic old farmer who predicted gloomily, "They'll never start her!" However, the steamboat did start. Its speed increased. Faster and faster it went, belching black billows of smoke from its funnel. The crowd on the riverbanks went wild with enthusiasm. But was this old pessimistic farmer impressed? Not on your life! He turned away, shaking his head, hardly able to believe what he saw, saying, "They'll never stop her!"

Many Christians are like that. They are always seeing the dark side. They are always gloomy. They are always negative. Paul suggested another approach to life, another spirit with which to face the challenges of each day. Paul said, "Rejoice!"

The word "rejoice" is in the imperative, reminding us that this disposition of joy, this optimistic spirit, can be and should be cultivated. Do not say we cannot approach life with that attitude. Do not claim we cannot face our challenges with that spirit. It would not have been commanded if it were not in the realm of possibility for the Christian. In the imperative mood, as a command, Paul said, "Rejoice!"

The word "always" reminds us that we are to approach life with this attitude all of the time, every day, not only in the good times, but in the dark times as well. How can we do that?

Commitment

The first step is commitment to the Lord. Paul did not simply say to rejoice. He said, "Rejoice in the Lord." In a similar vein the psalmist sang, "Happy is that people, whose God is the Lord" (Ps. 144:15, KJV), and the writer of Proverbs said, "Whoso trusteth in the Lord, happy is he" (Prov. 16:20, KJV). Real joy comes only in walking through life in harmony with God, for He is the source of real joy.

Lawrence of Arabia went to Paris after World War I with some of his Arab friends. They toured the city including the Arch of Triumph and Napoleon's Tomb. What really caught their eye were the faucets on the bathtubs in their hotel rooms. Lawrence's friends were amazed you could turn the handle and out came water. They spent hours just turning them on and off. When they were ready to leave Paris, Lawrence found his men in the bathroom trying to detach the faucets. When he asked why, they replied, "It is so dry in Arabia. We need those faucets so we can have all the water we want!" He had to explain to them that the effectiveness of the faucets depended on the immense water supply to which they were attached.

People are like that about joy. They want the faucets, but they miss the connection. Joy comes from the Lord. It is only as we are connected to Him that we can truly rejoice.

Contentment

Joy comes not only when we walk in harmony with God but also when we walk in harmony with ourselves. Contentment with who we are is a key ingredient in experiencing joy.

One of the classic dramas of American literature was "The Death of a Salesman," a play by Arthur Miller which featured Willie Loman, an ordinary, one-talent, small-time salesman who dreamed of hitting it big. He desperately desired a certain success in life but simply did not have the capacity to attain that level. He did possess some good qualities. However, he failed to actualize those because he was always trying to be something he was not. He committed suicide, and his son gave this brief epitaph of his father's life: "Poor Willie, he never really knew who he was."

That's the tragedy of life for many. We go through life chasing someone else's dream. Real joy comes when we recognize who we are, accept that, and find contentment in becoming the best we can be with the gifts God has given to us.

Compassion

We must not only walk in harmony with God and with ourselves, we must also walk in harmony with others. Joy comes when we give ourselves in service to others.

Two young men became friends in medical school, but they had quite different ambitions. One chose to establish a lucrative practice in his hometown. The other chose to bury his life in service to God on the mission field. Years later, the doctor who stayed home planned an around-the-world trip. He stopped off to see his friend from medical school. As they talked, the doctor from America was appalled at the primitive conditions and equipment the missionary doctor had to work with. Their conversation was interrupted as the missionary doctor left to perform surgery. When he returned, the American doctor asked, "Do you know how much you could have made from that surgery in the States?" "No," the missionary doctor replied. He was told the surgery would bring ten thousand dollars. The American doctor said, "And how much did you get here?" The missionary doctor replied, "A few pennies, and the smile of God!"

Real joy comes as we stand in the smile of God, and that happens when we give ourselves in service for others.

Stand Gently (v. 5)

Paul gave a fourth challenge. He said, "Let your forbearing spirit be known to all men" (v. 5). The word translated "forbearing spirit" is the Greek word, *epieikeshumon*. William Barclay calls it one of the most untranslatable of all Greek words. (2) It is translated "patience" in the *Wycliffe* translation, "forbearance" in the *Revised Standard Version*, "magnanimity" in the *New English Bible*, "gentleness" in the *New International Version*, "moderation" in the *King James Version*.

What does this word mean? It is the quality of going beyond the letter of the law, of going beyond justice. A forbearing spirit is convinced it is better to suffer wrong than to inflict wrong. A forbearing spirit is willing to give other people the benefit of the doubt.

When I studied this word I thought of Isabell and Price Morton, members of my former church in Atlanta, Georgia, a few years ago. They never met anyone they did not help. They would give money, a job, clothes, food, or encouragement to everybody who asked, and many times these people took advantage of their generosity. I once asked Price, "Why do you do that? Why do you let so many people take advantage of you?" He answered, 'I'd rather help a hundred people who don't need it than to miss helping one who does need it."

That's what a forbearing spirit is. It motivates us to treat people in the church better than they deserve, to always give them the benefit of the doubt, to suffer wrong rather than to inflict wrong.

Stand Strong (vv. 6-9)

In 1988 a song by Bobby McFerrin won three Grammy awards. It was not a song of intellectual depth. It was not a song with tremendous musical style. It was a simple song which repeated over twenty times this single phrase: "Don't Worry, Be Happy!" Such a simple song swept this country by storm because worry and anxiety are at the core of human existence today. Everyone is looking for an answer to help them overcome their anxiety and experience true joy in life. Everyone would like to be able not to worry and be happy. What anxieties are woven into the texture of life's pattern! Worry reigns over more human beings than any king who ever ruled. Therefore, we are somewhat shocked when Paul declared, "Be anxious for nothing." *The Living Bible* translates the opening phrase: "Don't worry about anything."

The word translated, "worry," in our text means to be pulled in two different directions, to have our energies divided. It comes from an old English root that means "to strangle." The kind of anxiety Paul was talking about is not a healthy preparedness for the future but an unhealthy fretting which pulls us in two directions and dilutes our energies. Worry immobilizes us in the present because we are focused on some event in the future. Worry is the interest paid on trouble before it is due. Paul said it has no place in the life of the Christian.

If Paul stopped there, we would write him off as an impractical idealist. Notice, however, Paul did not stop there. There is no period after that command but a comma, followed by Paul's suggestions on how that command can be carried out. How can we stand strong instead of giving in to anxiety?

Pray (vv. 6-7)

Paul's first suggestion was prayer. Paul said, "In everything by prayer and supplication with thanksgiving let your requests be made known to God." Paul used three different words to describe prayer. The general word, "prayer," carries with it the idea of adoration and worship. Supplication means an earnest sharing of our needs and problems with God. Thanksgiving means an expression of appreciation to God for who He is and what He does. Paul's emphasis was not on the Philippians's adoration of God. Nor was the emphasis on their laying their troubles before Him. The emphasis was on the thanksgiving with which they worshiped God and laid their troubles before Him. Thanksgiving was the key.

What does that mean? We should begin every prayer by praising God for being sovereign and sufficient. In every situation, "He who did not spare His own Son, but delivered Him up for us all . . . will . . . also with Him freely give us all things" (Rom. 8:32). To begin with that conviction is to end anxiety.

Anxiety says, "I am not able to deal with this situation." Thanksgiving says, "Praise God, He is able to deal with this situation, for all things are possible with Him." Worry is a sin, because it is based on the assumption that God is not able to take care of our lives. Worry is a theological problem, and the solution is to expand our concept of God to recognize He is able to do more than we could ever ask or even think.

When we pray, Paul said, "The peace of God, which surpasses all comprehension shall guard your hearts and your minds in Christ Jesus" (v. 7). The New Testament speaks of "peace with God" and the "peace of God." Peace with God is what we experience when we come into a right relationship with God through Jesus Christ. Paul spoke of this in Romans 5:1: "Therefore having been justified by faith, we have peace with God through our Lord Jesus Christ." The peace of God is what we experience as we live out our lives in that new relationship to God. That's what Paul referred to here in Philippians. Paul called it a peace "which surpasses all comprehension."

Those are the two choices which confront us. Our hearts can be torn apart by our anxiety. Or our hearts can be guarded by the peace of God which comes from prayer.

Refocus Our Minds (v. 8)

We not only need to pray. We also need to refocus our minds. Paul said, "Whatever is true, whatever is honorable, whatever is right, whatever is pure, whatever is lovely, whatever is of good repute, if there is any excellence and if anything worthy of praise, let your mind dwell on these things." The word translated "dwell" can also be translated "ponder" or "think." It means to calculate as when a workman takes careful measurements before he sets about his task.

Prayer is not all we need to do when our anxiety level rises. Prayer is certainly the first step, but certainly not the final step. After we bring God into the situation through prayer, then we need to carefully analyze the problem and determine what can be done. Bring our mind into it.

All of us have heard of and maybe have practiced counting sheep to deal with insomnia. Traditionally, we thought the serene pastoral setting through which the wooly creatures escaped was what relieved tension and led to sleep. Two Harvard psychologists have recently studied the matter and have concluded that the landscape has nothing to do with it. It is a matter of brain activity. Crudely speaking, the right side of the brain controls imagery and the left side, rational thought. Thus, visualizing sheep prevents the right hemisphere of the brain from producing anxiety producing imagery. The counting keeps the left hemisphere from straying into anxiety-producing thought. By keeping both sides of our brains busy, we drown out anxiety-producing visions and thoughts and thus, we are able to fall asleep. It's a matter of brain activity.

Two thousand years before these two men of science discovered that truth, a man of God suggested it to the Christians at Philippi. When we are faced by a threatening situation, we are to bring our minds into it. We should set our minds to work contemplating the resources that are ours and alternate courses that are open. We are to get our minds busy discovering what God and we can do to deal with this situation.

Act (v. 9)

Paul's third suggestion is in verse 9: "The things you have learned and received and heard and seen in me, practice these things."

The reason we worry so much is that our worry provides some underlying psychological payoffs. Our worry becomes an excuse for inactivity. "I can't do anything," we say, "I'm too worried." Thus, we do not have to take the risk that invariably accompanies action. It is easier to worry than to be an active, involved person. This points to the third antidote for worry: action. Many people spend their time stewing without doing. Paul suggested doing something about the things that worry us.

A little girl's brother built a trap to catch birds. She loved birds and was worried about what would happen to them. So this is what she did. She prayed that God would not let her brother catch any birds in his trap. Then she went out and kicked it to pieces! This is a simple illustration of what Paul wrote. When faced by a situation that threatens us with anxiety we are to: bring God into it; set our mind to work analyzing our resources and alternatives; and then do something. When we put our lives into action, we have entered the pathway which will lead us away from anxiety.

For Discussion

1. Do you think it is lonely in the church? How can we make strangers and new Christians feel more at home?

2. Remember some experience in the past when God enabled you to stand firm in the midst of a difficult situation. Share with the group.

3. Which ingredient is more important for experiencing joy: commitment, contentment, or compassion?

4. Do you know someone with a "forbearing spirit"? If so, describe that person to the group.

5. What are the antidotes to anxiety? Is one more important than the others? Which has been most helpful to you?

13 | The Christian Life

Philippians 4:10-23

William Borden was a young man, born into a wealthy American family and trained at Yale University and Princeton Seminary, who gave his life to the service of Christ. As a young man, William Borden was sent on a trip around the world. He came back from that trip with the world on his heart, and he decided to give his life to share Jesus Christ with the world. This was not only an ambition for the future, but also an ambition which motivated him all through his college years.

As an undergraduate at Yale, Borden was instrumental in organizing the Yale Hope Mission. He then financed most of its earlier work and was personally involved every week in helping the down and out find new hope in Christ. As a seminary student, Borden was involved in the work of the National Bible Institute in New York, and then during the summer he directed the work of the Bible Institute in Chicago. At the age of twenty-two, he was asked to serve on the council of the North American branch of the China Inland Mission, and played a vital role in the expansion of that work. As soon as he graduated from seminary, Borden set off on a three-month travel schedule throughout the United States to support the Student Volunteer Movement. His ordination at Moody Church in Chicago on September 9, 1912, marked the beginning of what he hoped would be a long life of missionary service directed toward the Islamic people, whom he considered the most neglected by Christian efforts.

The ultimate destination for this dedicated, gifted young missionary was a far-off province in northwest China called Kansu where three million Muslims lived. On his way to China, Borden stayed in Cairo, Egypt, for several months to learn more about the Muslim people. In Cairo, at the age of twenty-five with his whole life before him, he contracted cerebral meningitis. Within a month, William Borden was dead. In the final days of his life, Borden clung to the motto which had been the theme of his whole life: "No reserve, no retreat, no regrets."[1]

William Borden demonstrated in his life two ingredients most often missing in the Christian life today: contentment and confidence. Instead of contentment, there is among many Christians today a sense of discontent. Instead of confidence, there is among many Christians today an attitude of timidity. Nothing would be more helpful for us as Christians than to learn the secret of William Borden and to be able to face life, whether short or long, whether difficult or delightful, with his statement of commitment: "No reserve, no retreat, no regrets."

How can we do that? What are the resources and responsibilities of the Christian life? Paul painted a portrait of the Christian life in the closing verses of this Philippian Epistle.

The Contentment of the Christian Life (vv. 10-12)

Paul began with a word of thanksgiving to the Philippians. A strong bond of affection existed between the Philippian Christians and Paul. We feel it all the way through this Philippian letter. In prison, in isolation from other people, perhaps Paul had begun to doubt the affection of the Philippians. Absence does not always make the heart grow fonder. Sometimes it creates doubt and uncertainty about love. Apparently, a messenger came to Paul with a gift from the Philippians, reminding him of their love, and he expressed his gratitude to them for their generosity.

Paul's main concern, however, was not to thank the Philippians but to explain to them the source of his contentment. Paul's statement in verses 11-12 is one of the most remarkable statements he ever made. We learn several truths from Paul's statement about contentment.

Internal Basis Rather than an External Basis (v. 11)

Contentment is not based on outward circumstances but on inward commitment. Paul said, "I have learned to be content in whatever circumstances I am." If Paul's contentment was based on his circumstances, he would not have experienced very much contentment in life, for his life was usually set in the context of unpleasant circumstances. After his conversion, Paul went from one unpleasant circumstance to

another. Consider the scriptural testimony to this fact in the Book of
Acts.

> And when many days had elapsed, the Jews plotted together to do away
> with him, but their plot became known to Saul. And they were also watch-
> ing the gates day and night so that they might put him to death (9:23-24).
>
> But Jews came from Antioch and Iconium, and having won over the
> multitudes, they stoned Paul and dragged him out of the city, supposing
> him to be dead 14:19).
>
> And the crowd rose up together against them, and the chief magistrates
> tore their robes off them; and proceeded to order them to be beaten with
> rods. And when they had inflicted many blows upon them, they threw
> them into prison (16:22-23).
>
> But when the Jews of Thessalonica found out that the word of God had
> been proclaimed by Paul in Berea also, they came there likewise, agitating
> and stirring up the crowds (17:13).
>
> But while Gallio was proconsul of Achaia, the Jews with one accord
> rose up against Paul and brought him before the judgment seat (18:12).
>
> And there he spent three months, . . . when a plot was formed against
> him by the Jews (20:3).

Paul never had many pleasant circumstances, yet Paul could say, "I
have learned to be content in whatever circumstances I am." Why? Because his contentment did not come from circumstances but from commitment. Paul made this commitment: "For to me, to live is Christ"
(Phil. 1:21). That commitment was the source of his contentment.

Spiritual Basis Rather than a Material Basis (v. 12)

Contentment does not come from material prosperity but from spiritual security. Paul said, "I know how to get along with humble means,
and I also know how to live in prosperity."

If contentment came from material prosperity, we would expect those
who are the richest to be the most content. However, this is not the case.
Howard Hughes, for example, was one of the world's richest men. Yet,
he suffered from growing paranoia the last years of his life and lived in
almost total isolation. Material prosperity did not bring contentment to
him. Material prosperity, by itself, never does.

A novelist had one of his characters say, "We took what we wanted until we no longer wanted what we took." That is the ultimate end of a life devoted solely to the accumulation of material wealth.

In contrast, Paul gave up everything which the world depends on for contentment. Yet, he could say, "I have learned to be content in whatever circumstances I am." Why? Because his contentment did not come from the material but from the spiritual. Paul made this decision: "But whatever things were gain to me, those things I have counted as loss for the sake of Christ" (Phil. 3:7). That was the secret of his contentment.

From Christ Rather than from People (v. 11)

Contentment does not come from people but from Christ. We see this, not in any particular statement Paul made, but in Paul's word which is translated "content." The word is *autarkeia* which means "entirely self-sufficient" or "self-contained." The word describes a person who is sufficient apart from a relationship with any other person.

One of the most important elements in life is to have friends. I cannot imagine what life would be like if we had to live it all alone. Paul seemed to have a special knack for making friends. All the way through his letters we read of his affection toward and his prayer for his friends. But Paul was not dependent on those friends for his contentment. His contentment did not depend on any human relationship. He found his contentment in Christ.

We should be thankful for friends, but if we depend on friends for our contentment, we are headed for disappointment, because people are inevitably going to let us down. Sometimes, the people we love the deepest and trust the most let us down. Sometimes, our best friends let us down. Sometimes, those who believe in us and support us the most let us down.

Paul's primary relationship in life was his relationship with Christ. Paul said about his relationships, "I count all things to be loss in view of the surpassing value of knowing Christ Jesus my Lord" (Phil. 3:8). That relationship was the secret of his contentment.

To experience contentment in life, we need to follow the pattern of Paul. We need to make a commitment to Christ that will see us through all the changing circumstances of our life. We need to focus our attention on spiritual development rather than material accumulation. We need to make our relationship with Jesus Christ the primary relationship of our life.

The Confidence of the Christian Life (v13)

In verse 13, Paul turned to another important characteristic of the Christian life: confidence. Paul said, "I can do all things through Him who strengthens me." What a marvelous testimony for a Christian to give. How different from many of us today who limp from one spiritual defeat to another with the testimony, "I am just trying to serve Jesus in my own weak way." How different from many of us today who exalt ourselves above other Christians with the testimony, "Listen to me, and I will tell you what to believe, and how to live, and what to do." Paul displayed neither weakness nor arrogance when he said, "I can do all things through Him who strengthens me." Rather, he displayed the kind of confidence that should characterize every Christian today.

The Source of This Confidence

The word translated "strengthens" is a rare word, but it is one that Paul used quite often. We find it in 1 Timothy 1:12: "I thank Christ Jesus our Lord, who has strengthened me." We find it in 2 Timothy 4:17: "But the Lord stood with me, and strengthened me." We find it in Ephesians 6:10: "Finally, be strong in the Lord, and in the strength of His might." The word means "to infuse strength" or "to put power into." This strength, then, was not something that Paul conjured up from within. Instead, it was a power that was infused into his life. Paul's statement in verse 13 was not an expression of self-confidence but of God confidence. The source of this power is Jesus Christ, who infuses this strength in us.

Several years ago a visitor to the World's Fair noticed a man, dressed in a brilliant gold suit, standing beside a hand pump. His arm was moving up and down and the water was gushing out of the pump. As he observed from a distance, the visitor said, "That man is really pumping that water." However, when he moved closer he discovered this was not a man but a dummy whose arm was tied on to the arm of the pump which was being operated by electricity. He discovered the man was not pumping the water. The water was pumping him!

That's the way it is with the Christian. People see us from a distance and exclaim, "That man really has power for God." However, when they come closer they realize we are not pumping out this power of God. Instead, it is pumping us. Paul recognized the source of his power so he declared, "I can do all things through Him who strengthens me."

The Result of This Confidence

The result is an ability to face every challenge of life. This is the way Phillips translates this verse: "I am ready for anything through the strength of the One who lives within me." This power makes us adequate to live life victoriously. The purpose is to enable the believer to more effectively serve Christ. The power of Christ in us is not for gratifying our own personal whims but for carrying out the will of God.

The most magnificent truth about this confidence-producing power is that it is available to every person who will yield himself to Christ, who will give himself to the service of Christ, and who will make the full surrender for Christ.

I heard a preacher tell the story of a young woman in an Eastern European country several years ago. She heard the gospel message and was converted. Her parents, who were communists, made her leave home. In the course of six months at school, she shared her testimony and seven students were won to the Lord. However, as a result she was expelled from the school. She took a job in a bakery and within the next six months she won ten of her fellow workers to Christ. She was fired from the job, and eventually exiled from her country. In her new country, she was instrumental in forming a new church. When someone asked her how she could do so much, she replied, "Little is much when God is in it."

That was Paul's testimony as well. Because of his relationship with the Lord, He had power to do what God called him to do.

The Cooperation of the Christian Life (vv. 14-18)

Paul was grateful for the generous gifts which the Philippians had given to him. He described three different dimensions of these gifts: to himself as the recipient in verses 14-16, to the givers in verse 17, and to God in verse 18.

To Himself (vv. 14-16)

In relationship to himself, the gifts provided by the Philippians led to relief and rejoicing. The gifts adequately met his needs, and Paul was deeply grateful for them.

Joe picked up the phone one night and the operator said, "Long distance for Joe Johnston." Suddenly, a voice broke in saying, "Joe, this is your old pal, Freddy. Listen, I'm stuck here in Chicago and need $500." Joe responded, "I can't hear you. Something must be wrong with the phone." "I need $500," Freddy shouted louder. "I still can't hear you," Joe said again. Just then the operator interrupted, "I can hear him," she said. "Fine," Joe replied, "You send him the $500."

Real friends are not like that. They listen and they try to meet your need. These Philippians were friends of Paul's. Consequently, they repeatedly sent gifts to him and Paul said these gifts met his need.

To the Givers (v.17)

In relationship to the Philippians, giving these gifts enriched them. Paul explained, "Not that I seek the gift itself, but I seek for the profit which increases to your account" (v. 17).

Maxey Jarman of Nashville, Tennessee, who died at the age of seventy-six, was an internationally known Christian businessman. He took a company from seventy-five employees to 75,000 employees. His company, Genesco, in the late 1960s, was the world's largest apparel company. During his heyday, Maxey Jarman gave away millions. He built churches around the world and gave generously to all kinds of Christian causes. Then, he experienced financial reverses. He lost his company and most of his personal fortune. During the darkest days of his financial crunch, he was asked by a personal friend if he ever thought of the millions he had given away. Jarman answered, "Of course I have, but remember I didn't lose a penny I gave away. I only lost what I kept."

That is the paradox of Christian discipleship. What we give, we keep. What we let go of, we hold onto. When we are willing to empty ourselves, we become full. That's what Paul wrote to the Philippians. He was grateful for their gifts to him because in giving these gifts to him, the Philippians enriched their own lives.

To God (v. 18)

In relationship to God, these gifts were pleasing. Paul described the gifts as "a fragrant aroma, an acceptable sacrifice, well-pleasing to God."

What is it that makes a gift pleasing to God? It is not the worth of the gift. It is not the effort in giving the gift. It is not the propriety with which the gift is given. It is the motive of the one who gives it. Because the Philippians gave their gift out of a heart of love, Paul was able to say about it: your gift was "an acceptable sacrifice, well-pleasing to God."

When Paul thought about the gifts which the Philippians had given him, gifts which had met his needs and enriched their lives, and pleased God, Paul was grateful. In fact, one of the reasons Paul wrote this epistle was to thank the Philippians for their graciousness to him.

The Conviction of the Christian Life (v. 19)

In verse 19, Paul changed his focus. In verses 14-18, Paul focused on the provisions of the Philippians for which he was grateful. In verse 19, Paul focused on the provisions of God. He said, "And my God shall supply all your needs according to His riches in glory in Christ Jesus." The conviction of the Christian life is that God will provide for every need of our lives.

This is the keynote address of Paul's Letter to the Philippians, for this promise in Philippians 4:19 is the foundation upon which the entire epistle is built. Chapter one reflects the joy in Paul's life. The reason for his joy was the realization God would supply all of his needs in Christ Jesus. Chapter 2 reveals the submissiveness in Paul's life. The reason for his submissiveness was Paul's conviction about the inexhaustible sufficiency of God. Chapter 3 focuses on the purpose of Paul's life. Why did Paul strain like an athlete for the mark of the high calling of God? Because God was one whom he could trust to meet all his needs. Chapter 4 shows the contentment in Paul's life. The reason for his contentment was that Paul had discovered the inalterable adequacy of God. His joy, his submissiveness, his purpose, his contentment—all are rooted in this declaration which is one of the Bible's greatest promises: "My God shall supply all your needs according to His riches in glory in Christ Jesus."

The Surety of the Provisions

Notice that Paul did not say "My God might supply," or "My God could supply," or "My God ought to supply." Paul said, "My God *shall* supply." Notice also that Paul did not say, "My God will supply all your wants," or "My God will supply all your desires," but "My God will supply all your *needs.*" That is a fantastic promise. God will supply all our needs. It is a promise for each one of us.

Shadrach, Meshach, and Abed-nego understood the surety of God's provisions. When Nebuchadnezzar demanded they bow down before the idol, these three Hebrews refused. The king threatened to throw them into the fiery furnace if they did not relent. Still they refused with the bold declaration, "If it be so, our God whom we serve is able to deliver us from the furnace of blazing fire" (Dan. 3:17). Then they added this further word: "But even if He does not, let it be known to you, O King, that we are not going to serve your gods or worship the golden image that you have set up" (v. 18). In the first phrase, they said, "God will provide what we want." In the second phrase they added, "If He does not provide what we want, we know that He will provide what we need. He will either deliver us from the fire or through the fire!"

Like these three spiritual heroes of the past, the apostle Paul declared his trust in God, "And my God shall supply all your needs according to His riches in glory in Christ Jesus."

The Scope of the Provisions

God's provisions are not only for each one of us. They are also for each area of need.

Do we need forgiveness? God promised to provide for that in 1 John 1:9: "If we confess our sins, He is faithful and righteous to forgive us our sins and to cleanse us from all unrighteousness."

Do we need fellowship with God? God promised to meet that need in John 14:23: "If anyone loves me," Jesus said, "He will keep my Word; and my Father will love him and We will come to him and make our abode with him."

Are we burdened by the weight of our load? God will provide for that, too. Jesus said, "Come to Me, all who are weary and heavy-laden, and I will give you rest" (Matt. 11:28).

Do we need help to overcome temptation? Again, the provisions of God are promised. The Bible says, "No temptation has overtaken you but such as is common to man; and God is faithful, who will not allow you to be tempted beyond that you are able, but with the temptation will provide the way of escape also, that you may be able to endure it" (1 Cor. 10:13).

Do we need help with worry? Read again the promise in verses 6 and 7 of this fourth chapter of Philippians. Instead of worrying, Paul suggested that "in everything by prayer and supplication with thanksgiving let your requests be made known to God, and the peace of God, which surpasses all comprehension, shall guard your hearts and your minds in Christ Jesus."

Do we need hope for tomorrow? Then hear the truth that James discovered: "Blessed is the man who perseveres under trial; for once he has been approved, he will receive the crown of life, which the Lord has promised to those who love Him" (Jas. 1:12).

We could go on need by need and Scripture by Scripture, but the point is clear. Whatever we need, God can and will supply that need. It is God's promise. This promise is not just a provision for the pious and the perfect. It is available to every Christian and it is sufficient for every need.

Someone once counted 7,487 promises by God to man in the Bible. That may or may not be an accurate count. I have not counted them. But however many promises there are in the Bible, every one is for us.

The Source of the Provisions

What is the source of these provisions? Listen again to what Paul said: "My God shall supply all your needs according to His riches in glory." Notice the contrast between verses 14-18 and verse 19. In verses 14-18, Paul talked about the provisions made for him through an offering the Philippian Christians sent him. He then contrasted that with the provisions of God. Paul declared, "You met one need I have, and I am thankful for that, but my God will meet all of my needs. You gave out of your poverty, but God will supply my need out of His riches in glory."

God has four accounts according to Scripture: the riches of His goodness (Rom. 2:4), the riches of His wisdom (11:33), the riches of His grace (Eph. 1:7), and the riches of His glory (v. 18). Out of the latter account

God supplies all our needs, and this source is incomparable, infinite, and inexhaustible.

Our financial institutions used to seem sound and secure, but now their resources are often depleted. Bountiful wells have supplied water for many villages, but at times, they have dried up. Vast acres of land have been productive and fertile, which now have become arid wastelands. Many mines, once producing valuable ore, are now exhausted. Some engineers say a time is coming when even our supply of oil will be depleted, and our mass transportation system will come to a screeching halt. In contrast to all of those depletable resources, God's resources are inexhaustible. When all the oil is gone, when the mines are closed, when all the land is wasted, when all the wells are dry, and when all the banks are defunct, God's account will be just as full and just as adequate as it is right now. It is a source which will never run dry. It is inexhaustible. Out of that source God will supply all our needs.

How can these provisions be ours? The key is in the last phrase. Paul said, "And my God shall supply all your needs according to His riches in glory in Christ Jesus." That phrase, "in Christ Jesus," takes this promise and brings it right down to where we live. For those of us who are in Christ Jesus, the treasures of God are right here with us. We don't have to stretch, search, or beg for them. All we have to do is open our hands and receive the spiritual riches Christ makes available to us. When we realize God will provide every need and when we begin to experience His provisions, then we can begin LIVING JOYFULLY.

For Discussion

1. What were the sources of Paul's contentment?
2. Who is the most contented person you know? What is his or her secret?
3. What is the difference between self-confidence and God-confidence?
4. What are some of the positive results of Christian giving?
5. What are some of the benefits God provides for us?

Notes

Chapter 1

1. Bill Adler, *Dear Pastor* (Nashville: Thomas Nelson, 1980), 59, 75, 109.
2. J. B. Lightfoot, *St. Paul's Epistle to the Philippians* (Grand Rapids, MI: Zondervan, 1953), 95.

Chapter 2

1. For more on this great man of prayer see Basil Miller, *George Muller: Man of Faith and Miracles* (Minneapolis: Dimension Books, 1941).
2. William Barclay, *A Spiritual Autobiography* (Grand Rapids, MI: William B. Eerdmans, 1975), 14.
3. Roy Honeycutt, "Claiming the Higher Ground," in *Pulpit Digest*, May-June, 1984, 33-34.
4. Warren Wiersbe, *Be Joyful* (Wheaton: Victor Books, 1974), 25-26.

Chapter 3

1. Viktor E. Frankl, *Man's Search for Meaning* (New York: Pocket Books, 1959), xi.
2. These experiences of Paul, described in Acts 21:17 to 28:31, are elaborated in Brian L. Harbour, *Living Expectantly: Acts* (Nashville: Broadman, 1990), 151-170.
3. Wiersbe, 32.

Chapter 4

1. Barclay, 9.
2. Wiersbe, 38
3. David B. Guralnik, ed. *Webster's New World Dictionary of the American Language* (Nashville: The Southwestern Company, 1972), 389.
4. Paul Powell, *When the Hurt Won't Go Away* (Wheaton: Victor Books, 1986), 118-19.
5. Tony Campolo, *The Kingdom of God Is a Party* (Dallas: Word, 1990), 129-30.

Chapter 5

1. Gary Collins, *The Magnificent Mind* (Waco: Word, 1985), 139.
2. Tim Hansel, *Holy Sweat* (Waco: Word, 1987), 104.
3. Paul Powell, *Why Me, Lord?* (Wheaton: Victor Books, 1981), 26.

Chapter 6

1. James E. Hightower, *Illustrating Paul's Letter to the Romans* (Nashville: Broadman, 1984), 113.

2. William Barclay, *The Letters to the Philippians, Colossians, and Thessalonians*, Revised (Philadelphia: The Westminster Press, 1975), 33.

3. Paul E. Boller, *Presidential Anecdotes* (New York: Penguin Books, 1981), 15.

4. James C. Humes, *Speakers' Treasury of Anecdotes About the Famous* (New York: Harper, 1978), 161.

Chapter 7

1. This classic has been produced by several different publishers. The volume I have was published by Fleming H. Revell Company with no date.

2. Dennis Waitley, *The Winner's Edge* (New York: Berkley Books, 1980), 20.

3. Larry King, *Tell It to the King* (New York: G. P. Putnam's Sons, 1988), 179.

4. Wiersbe, 54.

5. Gipsy Smith, *Best Sermons Delivered in Brooklyn* (New York: J. S. Ogilve Publishing Co., 1907), 242.

Chapter 8

1. Fred Craddock, *Philippians* (Atlanta: John Knox Press, 1985), 46.

2. *Webster's,* 753.

3. John W. Drakeford, *Wisdom for Today's Family* (Nashville: Broadman, 1978), 142.

4. Hightower, *Romans,* 10.

Chapter 9

1. Robert Schuller, *The Be (Happy) Attitudes* (Waco: Word, 1985), 60.

2. Barclay, *Philippians,* 76.

3. Webster, 438.

4. Barclay, *Philippians,* 50.

Chapter 10

1. Barclay, *Philippians,* 55.

Chapter 11

1. James Carter, *Help for the Evangelistic Preacher* (Nashville: Broadman, 1985), 97-98.

2. Paul Powell, *The Complete Disciple* (Wheaton: Victor Books, 1982), 54.

3. Stephen Brown, *If God is in Charge* (Nashville: Thomas Nelson, 1983), 164.

4. B.O. Baker, *The Lift of Love* (Nashville: Broadman, 1986), 126.

Chapter 12

1. Charles Swindoll, *Dropping Your Guard* (Waco: Word, 1983), p. 127.
2. Barclay, *Philippians,* 75.

Chapter 13

1. For a concise biography of this unique man of God see Mrs. Howard Taylor, *Borden of Yale* (Minneapolis: Bethany House Publishers, 1988).